Passing your PRINCE2® Exams

AXELOS
GLOBAL BEST PRACTICE

tso

a Williams Lea company

Published by TSO (The Stationery Office), part of Williams Lea, and available from:

Online
www.tsoshop.co.uk

Mail, Telephone, Fax & E-mail
TSO
PO Box 29, Norwich, NR3 1GN
Telephone orders/General enquiries: 0333 202 5070
Fax orders: 0333 202 5080
E-mail: customer.services@tso.co.uk
Textphone 0333 202 5077

TSO@Blackwell and other Accredited Agents

ISBN 9780113316694

Printed in the United Kingdom for The Stationery Office.
Material is FSC certified and produced using ECF pulp, sourced from fully sustainable forests.

P003004553 11/19 C5

Contents

Foreword

The purpose of this guide is to help people prepare for their PRINCE2® examinations. It is also intended for those who have decided to maintain their practitioner status by taking an examination rather than by collecting continuous professional development (CPD) points via AXELOS My PRINCE2 membership. It may serve as a refresher for those who need to regain their qualification or who wish to test their understanding of the revised guidance, especially the additional elements on tailoring. This publication is not intended to be a substitute for the guidance found in *Managing Successful Projects with PRINCE2*, but to work alongside that publication and show how your knowledge will be tested.

The examinations are designed to test your knowledge of PRINCE2 at two levels. Firstly, to confirm your awareness and understanding of the basic PRINCE2 vocabulary and establish a foundational level. Secondly, at practitioner level, to confirm your ability to apply PRINCE2 to a given test scenario and demonstrate your ability to tailor the method appropriately.

This publication will be helpful to those preparing to undertake formal PRINCE2 training via an accredited training organization, self-study or a distance learning approach. It is important to find a learning style that suits you best. Whichever way is best for you, this book will help you prepare for, and become comfortable with, both the foundation and practitioner level examination formats.

I would like to wish you good luck not only in preparing for your PRINCE2 examinations but in using PRINCE2 throughout your career.

Margo Leach

Chief product officer, AXELOS Global Best Practice

Chief examiner's foreword

Project management is now recognized and accepted as a profession with a maturity that demands professional standards and training. The PRINCE2 qualification scheme has evolved with the profession and has a history of development and improvement that has led to its adoption by project management professionals worldwide.

In 2017, the sixth edition of *Managing Successful Projects with PRINCE2* was published and the qualification scheme and associated examinations were updated at the same time. The sixth edition explains what you should do for your project to be considered a PRINCE2 project. In addition, it has introduced guidance on how to tailor PRINCE2 to different project environments, making it even more valuable to individuals and organizations alike. *Passing your PRINCE2 Exams* (replacing *Passing the PRINCE2 Examinations* published in 2009) has been developed to support candidates intending to take the foundation and/or practitioner examinations, taking into account the sixth edition as well as providing advice and guidance on how to approach the examinations.

I recommend this guidance to all candidates intending to take a PRINCE2 examination in order to familiarize themselves with the way that questions are asked, the structure of the examinations as a whole, and to give themselves the best chance of success when taking those examinations.

Michelle Rowland

PRINCE2 chief examiner

About AXELOS

AXELOS is a joint venture company co-owned by the UK Government's Cabinet Office and Capita plc. It is responsible for developing, enhancing and promoting a number of best-practice methodologies used globally by professionals working primarily in project, programme and portfolio management, IT service management and cyber resilience.

The methodologies, including ITIL®, PRINCE2®, MSP® and the new collection of cyber resilience best-practice products, RESILIA™, are adopted in more than 150 countries to improve employees' skills, knowledge and competence in order to make both individuals and organizations work more effectively.

In addition to globally recognized qualifications, AXELOS equips professionals with a wide range of content, templates and toolkits through its membership scheme, its professional development programme and its online community of practitioners and experts.

Visit www.axelos.com for the latest news about how AXELOS is making organizations more effective and registration details to join the AXELOS online community. If you have specific queries or requests, or would like to be added to the AXELOS mailing list, please contact ask@axelos.com.

Publications

The PRINCE2 product suite comprises a range of core and supplementary guidance to support you on your project management journey.

For information on the PRINCE2 certification scheme and to purchase digital or hard copies of the guidance, visit:

- What is PRINCE2? http://tiny.cc/what-is-PRINCE2
- *Managing Successful Projects with PRINCE2*: http://tiny.cc/Prince2manual
- *Directing Successful Projects with PRINCE2*: http://tiny.cc/DSP
- *PRINCE2 Handbook:* http://tiny.cc/prince2handbook

PRINCE2 also offers essential interactive digital resources to enhance your learning experience. Maximize your chances of exam success with the official PRINCE2 Foundation app and use smart tabs to locate relevant sections in your PRINCE2 manual while accessing applicable online materials using QR codes.

Details can be found at:

- PRINCE2 Foundation app: http://tiny.cc/prince2app
- PRINCE2 SmartTabs: http://tiny.cc/prince2smarttabs

You may also wish to consider the PRINCE2 Agile guide and certification which integrates PRINCE2 methodology with Agile frameworks, behaviours, tools and techniques. See:

- PRINCE2 Agile project management certifications: http://tiny.cc/prince2agilecertify
- *PRINCE2 Agile*: http://tiny.cc/Prince2agile

Contact information

Full details on how to contact AXELOS can be found at:

https://www.axelos.com

For further information on certification and training, please visit:

https://www.axelos.com/certifications

https://www.axelos.com/find-a-training-provider

For all other enquiries, please email:

ask@axelos.com

Acknowledgements

Authors

Written and compiled from Sue Taylor's original text by Mike Acaster, Richard Bell, Neil Glover, Michelle Rowland and Allan Thomson.

This content has been amended to take into account:

- changes to *Managing Successful Projects with PRINCE2* 6th edition (TSO, 2017)
- changes to the foundation and practitioner exam syllabus and format
- advances in examination environment options, notably on-screen and non-classroom-based exams.

Special thanks are due to QA Training Limited and PeopleCert for providing materials recreated in this publication.

Reviewers

Lorna Gilbert and Michelle Rowland.

1

The PRINCE2 qualifications

1 The PRINCE2 qualifications

PRINCE2 (PRojects IN Controlled Environments) is a project management method which is used extensively in more than 150 countries around the world, and its take-up grows daily. It was originally conceived in the 1970s and since then has grown and developed into the project management method of choice for many international organizations, being widely considered as the world's leading method. It is based on experience drawn from thousands of projects, and from the contributions of numerous people involved in projects, including project managers, project teams, academics, trainers, consultants and others. It is generic and can be applied to any project regardless of project scale, type, complexity, organization, region or culture.

PRINCE2 is part of a suite of guidance offered by AXELOS, which is aimed at helping organizations and individuals manage their projects, programmes and services consistently and effectively. *Passing your PRINCE2 Exams* has been drafted taking into account the changes made to:

- *Managing Successful Projects with PRINCE2* (6th edition) – hereafter referred to as the PRINCE2 manual
- the updated syllabus aligned with the revised practical guidance
- examination environment options, notably on-screen and non-classroom-based exams
- the updated exam structure at foundation and practitioner levels.

1.1 Purpose of the guide

This guide gives an overview of both the foundation and practitioner qualifications and is designed to help you prepare for the examinations. It has been updated to reflect the changes in the examinations introduced alongside the release of the sixth edition of the PRINCE2 manual in 2017. It contains:

- details of the PRINCE2 syllabuses, showing the different assessment criteria used, together with the appropriate learning outcomes

- an outline of the structure and format of the foundation and practitioner examinations
- a sample paper for each examination, together with rationales for the correct answers
- a description of the different question types which may be included in each examination
- further comments from the chief examiner on how to answer some of the questions with simplified explanations.

This guide does not attempt to provide you with details of the PRINCE2 method itself. You can find these in the PRINCE2 manual, which is essential reading if you wish to sit the examinations and obtain either foundation or practitioner qualified status.

1.2 How to prepare for your exam

Note that, in the case of taking an online exam via remote proctor, some organizations may offer an invigilated exam at one of their exam centres.

Figure 1.1 shows a variety of ways that you can prepare for your exam.

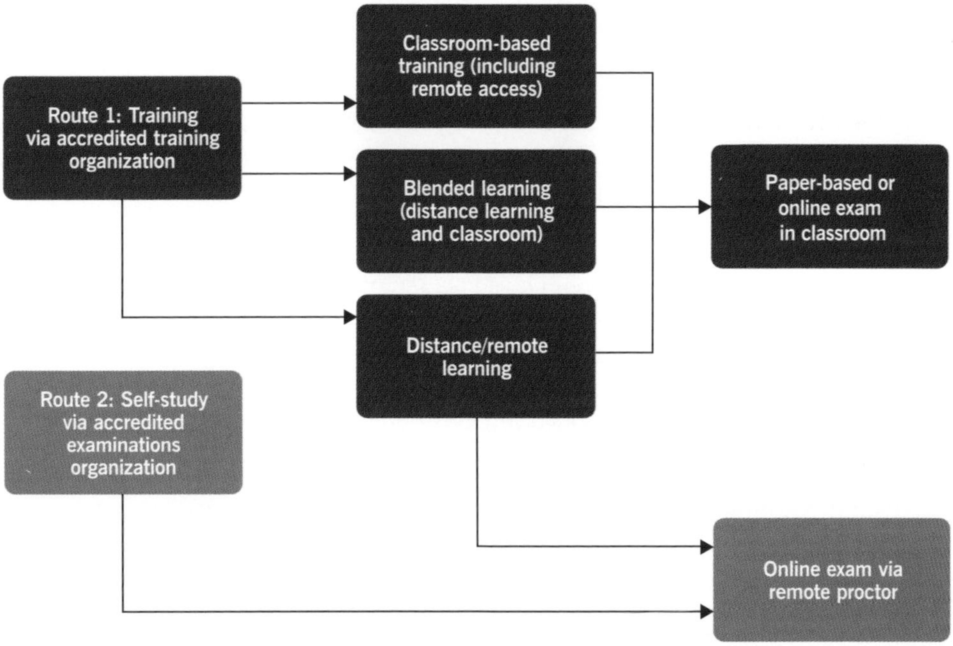

Figure 1.1 Study paths to your exam

To prepare for your exam, there are two main routes:

- Study with an accredited training organization (ATO). The cost of the course will typically include your exams and may comprise:
  - classroom-based study (including joining via remote access)
  - blended learning – a mix of distance learning/e-learning with some classroom-based study
  - distance learning/e-learning
- Self-study, in which case you will need to find an accredited examinations organization which will typically offer you an online exam (some organizations may offer an invigilated exam at one of their exam centres). You can download sample papers from the AXELOS website to prepare for your examinations. They are also included in this publication in sections 2.5 and 3.7.

If you are taking a PRINCE2 qualification for the first time and/or are new to project management, it is recommended that you study with an ATO if possible as this will ensure that you obtain a more rounded understanding of the method.

1.3 How to take your exam

Depending on the route that you choose to study PRINCE2, you will take your exam in one of the following three ways:

- Paper-based in a classroom supervised by an invigilator as part of your accredited training
- Online in a classroom supervised by an invigilator as part of your accredited training
- Online at a location/time of your choice via remote proctor. This is the way you will typically take your exam if you have self-studied, done a distance/remote learning course or if you are re-sitting an exam for whatever reason.

Figure 1.2 summarizes the steps involved in taking your online exam.

No matter which route you are using to take your exam (online or paper-based), you will need to set up a PeopleCert account. This only takes a few minutes, but you will not be able to take your exam without it. Once you have set up your account, you will also need to register for your exam(s). You should receive a voucher code from your accredited organization to enable you to do this.

If you are taking the online exam via remote proctor you will need to book a time. You will need to have a quiet location for your exam and a device with a webcam.

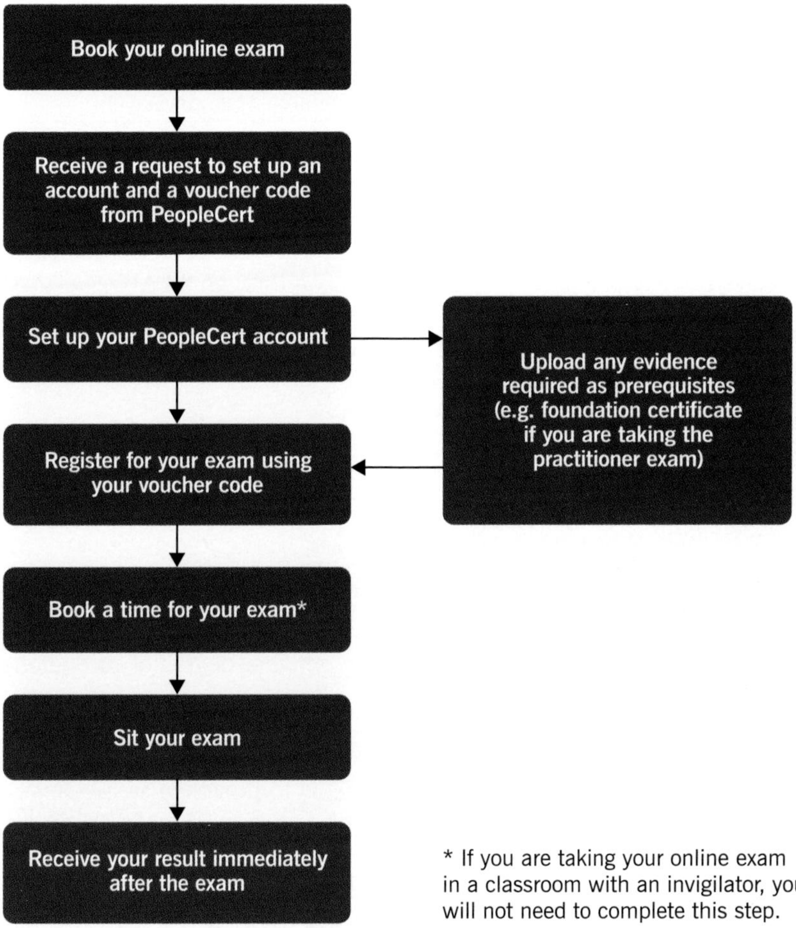

* If you are taking your online exam in a classroom with an invigilator, you will not need to complete this step.

Figure 1.2 How to take your online exam

The proctor will want to check that the room is suitable and clear of any materials that are not permitted in an exam room. It is normally recommended that you use a personal device for this as you will need to download some remote proctor software which may not be possible on a device owned by an employer.

If you are taking the practitioner exam, you will need to first upload a copy of your PRINCE2 foundation certificate to your PeopleCert profile. Only foundation certificates achieved with the PRINCE2 5th edition or later will be accepted as a prerequisite. Your practitioner exam result will not be released until an acceptable prerequisite has been uploaded, regardless of the result of your practitioner exam.

If you passed your foundation exam after January 2018, or with PeopleCert at an earlier date, your foundation certificate should already be available on your PeopleCert profile page. For information on valid prerequisite certifications from other organizations, see Chapter 3.

1.4 Overview of the PRINCE2 qualifications

The PRINCE2 manual provides guidance on the principles, themes and processes used to manage projects, including how to tailor the method to suit any environment. PRINCE2 is supported by:

- online, classroom-based or remote access training through an ATO
- a two-tier qualification scheme:
  - foundation level to determine whether candidates have understood the concept and intent of PRINCE2
  - practitioner level to assess whether the candidates are able to analyse situations and apply the appropriate PRINCE2-based response within a given scenario.

A classification widely used when designing assessments for certification and education is *Bloom's Taxonomy of Educational Objectives*. This classifies learning objectives into six ascending levels, each defining a higher degree of competencies and skills.[1]

The PRINCE2 learning outcomes assessment model on which the exams are based uses Bloom's taxonomy. The purpose of the model is to provide a simple and systematic means for assessing and classifying the learning outcomes for the PRINCE2 exams.

The model is used during development of the syllabus to help identify the individual learning outcomes and assign each of these to a learning or Bloom's level (BL). These form the basis of the syllabus topics, with the classification contributing to the assessment of a question's difficulty in the exams. This structured approach helps to ensure that:

- a clear boundary exists in learning level content between the different qualification levels
- learning outcomes are documented consistently across different areas of the PRINCE2 manual
- exam questions and papers are created to a consistent level of difficulty.

The model presented in Table 1.1 is a specific interpretation of this generic model which has been created for the PRINCE2 qualifications.

1 Bloom, B.S. (ed.), Engelhart, M.D., Furst, E.J., Hill, W.H. and Krathwohl, D.R. (1956) *Taxonomy of Educational Objectives. Handbook I: The Cognitive Domain*. New York: David McKay Co.

Table 1.1 Bloom's level definitions used by the PRINCE2 assessment model

Bloom's levels		
1	Recall (previously referred to as knowledge)	Able to identify, recognize and recall facts from the PRINCE2 manual, including terms, concepts, principles, themes, processes and responsibilities
2	Describe (previously referred to as comprehension)	Able to describe and explain the principles, processes, themes, the project's environment, management products and roles
3	Apply (previously referred to as application)	Able to show within the given scenario the ability to appropriately apply: ● the PRINCE2 principles ● the PRINCE2 themes ● the PRINCE2 processes ● the PRINCE2 management products ● tailoring of the PRINCE2 themes, processes and management products to meet the context.
4	Analyse (previously referred to as analysis)	Able to show through the examination, appraisal and critique of completed management products and project events within the given scenario
5	Evaluate (previously referred to as evaluation)	Not used in PRINCE2
6	Create (previously referred to as synthesis)	Not used in PRINCE2

Please note that the Bloom nomenclature has changed and the older terms are also shown here for those who may be more familiar with them.

Both the foundation and practitioner syllabuses are presented in a common format as can be seen in Chapters 2 and 3. The examination format differs for the two exams; a summary of the differences is provided in Table 1.2.

Table 1.2 Summary of the differences in examination format

Examination	Examination format (5th edition)	Examination format (6th edition)
Foundation	1 hour	1 hour
	75 questions	60 questions
	Multiple choice	Multiple choice
	50% pass mark	55% pass mark (33 out of 60)
	Closed book	Closed book
Practitioner	2.5 hours	2.5 hours
	Objective test	Objective test
	8 questions (10 marks per question)	68 questions: 35 standard multiple choice and 33 matching (3 sub-questions per matching question)
	80 possible marks	68 possible marks
	55% pass mark	55% pass mark (38 out of 68 marks or higher)
	Open book (PRINCE2 manual only)	Open book (PRINCE2 manual only)

2

Foundation qualification

2 Foundation qualification

The purpose of the PRINCE2 foundation examination is to assess whether the candidate can demonstrate sufficient recall and understanding of the PRINCE2 project management method, as described in the syllabus below, to be awarded the PRINCE2 foundation qualification.

The target audience for this qualification is:

- project managers and aspiring project managers
- other key staff involved in the design, development and delivery of projects, including:
  - project board members (e.g. the executive sponsoring the project)
  - team managers (e.g. product delivery managers)
  - project assurance (including those from quality assurance or audit teams)
  - project support (e.g. project and programme office personnel)
  - operational line managers/staff (such as those who will be ensuring a smooth transition of the changes into business as usual and realizing the benefits).

2.1 Foundation syllabus

Table 2.1 summarizes the foundation syllabus, learning outcomes, assessment criteria, Bloom's levels and marks. The syllabus is also available as a downloadable PDF at AXELOS.com.

Table 2.1 Foundation examination: learning outcomes, assessment criteria, Bloom's levels and marks

Learning outcome		Assessment criteria*			BL	Marks
1	Understand key concepts relating to projects and PRINCE2	1.1	**Recall:** a. The definition and characteristics of a project (2.1) b. The six aspects of project performance to be managed (2.3) c. The integrated elements of PRINCE2: principles, themes, processes and the project environment (1.1) d. What makes a project a PRINCE2 project (1.3)		1	3
		1.2	**Describe:** a. The features and benefits of PRINCE2 (1) b. The customer/supplier context on which PRINCE2 is based, including considerations when undertaking projects in a commercial environment (2.5, 2.5.4)		2	2
2	Understand how the PRINCE2 principles underpin the PRINCE2 method	2.1	**Explain** the PRINCE2 principles: a. Continued business justification (3.1) b. Learn from experience (3.2) c. Defined roles and responsibilities (3.3) d. Manage by stages (3.4) e. Manage by exception (3.5) f. Focus on products (3.6) g. Tailor to suit the project (3.7)		2	7
		2.2	**Explain:** a. Which aspects of a project can be tailored b. Who is responsible c. How tailoring decisions are documented (4.3.1–4.3.2)		2	1
3	Understand the PRINCE2 themes and how they are applied throughout the project	3.1	**Business case theme**			
			3.1.1	**Explain** the purpose of: a. Managing business justification (6.1) b. Key management products: ● business case (A.2.1) ● benefits management approach (A.1.1)	2	1
			3.1.2	**Describe** what PRINCE 2 requires, as a minimum, for managing business justification (6.2 excl. subsections)	2	1
			3.1.3	**Define** key concepts related to business justification, and the differences between them for: ● outputs ● outcomes ● benefits ● dis-benefits (6.1, Fig. 6.1)	1	1

Table continues

Table 2.1 *continued*

Learning outcome		Learning outcome			BL	Marks
3	Understand the PRINCE2 themes and how they are applied throughout the project *continued*	3.2	**Organization theme**			
			3.2.1	**Explain** the purpose of: a. Managing organization (7.1) b. Key management products: ● communication management approach (A.5.1)	2	1
			3.2.2	**Describe** what PRINCE 2 requires, as a minimum, for managing organization (7.2 excl. subsections, Fig. 7.3)	2	1
			3.2.3	**Describe** the roles and responsibilities of the: a. Project board (7.2.1.1) b. Executive (7.2.1.2) c. Senior user (7.2.1.3) d. Senior supplier (7.2.1.4) e. Project assurance (7.2.1.5) f. Change authority (7.2.1.6) g. Project manager (7.2.1.7) h. Team manager (7.2.1.8) i. Project support (7.2.1.9), including j. Those roles which can be combined (7.2.1.10)	BL2	4
			3.2.4	**Explain** key concepts related to organization: a. Stakeholder (7.1) b. The three project interests and how these are represented within the four levels of management (7.1, Fig. 7.1, Fig. 7.2)	2	1

Learning outcome	Learning outcome			BL	Marks
	3.3	**Quality theme**			
		3.3.1	**Explain** the purpose of: a. Managing quality (8.1) b. Key management products: • project product description (A.21.1) • product description (A.17.1) • quality register (A.23.1) • quality management approach (A.22.1)	2	2
		3.3.2	**Describe** what PRINCE 2 requires, as a minimum, for managing quality (8.2 excl. subsections)	2	1
		3.3.3	**Explain** key concepts related to quality, and the differences between them: a. Quality planning and quality control (8.1.1) b. Project assurance and quality assurance (8.1.1) c. Customer quality expectations and acceptance criteria (8.1, 8.3.6, 8.3.8)	2	1
	3.4	**Plans theme**			
		3.4.1	**Explain** the purpose of: a. Managing plans (9.1) b. Types of plan: • project plan (9.2.1.1, A.16.1) • stage plan (9.2.1.2, A.16.1) • exception plan (9.2.1.3, A.16.1) • team plan (9.2.1.4, A.16.1)	2	1
		3.4.2	**Describe** the PRINCE2 minimum requirements for managing plans (9.2 excl. subsections)	2	1
		3.4.3	**Recall**: a. The steps in the recommended approach to planning (Fig. 9.2), including b. The steps in the recommended product-based planning technique (9.3.1.1–9.3.1.7)	1	2
			Explain: c. The factors to consider when structuring the project into management stages (9.3.1.1)	2	1

Table continues

Table 2.1 *continued*

Learning outcome		Learning outcome			BL	Marks
3	Understand the PRINCE2 themes and how they are applied throughout the project *continued*	3.5	**Risk theme**			
			3.5.1	**Explain** the purpose of: a. Managing risk, including the purpose of a risk budget (10.1, 10.3.7) b. Key management products: • risk management approach (A.24.1) • risk register (A.25.1)	2	1
			3.5.2	**Describe** what PRINCE 2 requires, as a minimum, for managing risk (10.2 excl. subsections)	2	1
			3.5.3	**Define** key concepts related to risk, and the differences between them: a. A risk: threat or opportunity (10.1) b. Recommended risk response types (Tab. 10.3) c. Risk owner and risk actionee (10.4.4) d. Cause, event and effect (10.4.1.2) e. Risk probability, risk impact and risk proximity (10.4.2.1)	1	2
			3.5.4	**Describe** the risk management procedure (10.3.2, 10.4.1–10.4.5)	2	1
		3.6	**Change theme**			
			3.6.1	**Explain** the purpose of: a. Managing change, including the purpose of a change budget (11.1, 11.3.6) b. Key management products: • change control approach (A.3.1) • configuration item record (A.6.1) • issue register (A.12.1) • issue report (A.13.1) • product status account (A.18.1)	2	1
			3.6.2	**Describe** what PRINCE2 requires, as a minimum, for managing change (11.2 excl. subsections)	2	1
			3.6.3	**Describe**: a. Types of issue (11.1, Tab. 11.1) b. The recommended issue and change control procedure (Fig. 11.1, 11.4.1.1–11.4.1.5)	2	1

Learning outcome		Learning outcome			BL	Marks
		3.7	**Progress theme**			
			3.7.1	**Explain** the purpose of: a. Controlling progress (12.1) b. Key management products: ● daily log (A.7.1) ● lessons log (A.14.1, 12.2.2.3) ● lessons report (A.15.1) ● work package (A.26.1, 12.2.2.1) ● end stage report (A.9.1, 12.2.2.4) ● end project report (A.8.1, 12.2.2.4) ● checkpoint report (A.4.1, 12.2.2.4) ● highlight report (A.11.1, 12.2.2.4) ● exception report (A.10.1, 12.2.3)	2	2
			3.7.2	**Describe** what PRINCE2 requires, as a minimum, for controlling progress (12.2 excl. subsections)	2	1
			3.7.3	**Explain** key concepts related to progress: a. Event-driven and time-driven controls (12.2.2) b. Tolerances and exceptions, including how tolerances are set and exceptions are reported (12.2.1, Fig. 12.1, 12.2.3)	2	2
4	Understand the PRINCE2 processes and how they are carried out throughout the project	4.1	**Explain** the purpose of the PRINCE2 processes: a. Starting up a project (14.1), including the purpose of the project brief (A.19.1) b. Directing a project (15.1), including the purpose of the project initiation documentation (A.20.1) c. Initiating a project (16.1) d. Controlling a stage (17.1) e. Managing product delivery (18.1) f. Managing a stage boundary (19.1) g. Closing a project (20.1)		2	6
		4.2	**Explain** the objectives of the PRINCE2 processes (14.2, 15.2, 16.2, 17.2, 18.2, 19.2, 20.2)		2	5
		4.3	**Explain** the context of the PRINCE2 processes (14.3, 15.3, 16.3, 17.3, 18.3, 19.3, 20.3)		2	5

* Primary references to the PRINCE2 manual are given in parentheses. The verb (in bold type) for each assessment criterion indicates the Bloom's level (e.g. 'Identify', 'Define', 'Recall', 'Recognize' indicate Level 1 Basic recall and recognition; 'Describe', 'Explain' indicate Level 2 Understanding/comprehension).

2.2 Foundation question types

The PRINCE2 foundation exam is an objective test exam (OTE). OTEs are ideally suited to the multiple choice format of the PRINCE2 foundation exam. One advantage of OTEs is that they free the exam from any bias due to interpretation by a marker as the correct answer is predetermined. Therefore, there is a right answer and all other options are wrong. This type of exam is in contrast to the subjective exam questions typified by a written essay response. All 60 questions are objective test questions, which present four options from which one option should be selected. Distractors (wrong answers) are options that candidates with incomplete knowledge or skill might choose. These are generally plausible responses relating to the syllabus area being examined. There are four types of multiple choice questions used in the foundation exam:

- standard
- missing-word
- list (two correct items)
- negative.

Note that negative multiple choice questions are only used on very rare occasions when the manual specifically states that something should not be done.

Primary references to the PRINCE2 manual are given in parentheses.

2.2.1 Examples of standard multiple choice questions

Which individual role is ultimately accountable for the project?

A Executive

B Project manager

C Senior supplier

D Senior user

The answer is A. This is because, although the project board has collective responsibility for the project, the executive, supported by the senior user and senior supplier, is ultimately accountable for the project's success and is the key decision maker (7.2.1.2).

How is the 'learn from experience' principle applied?

A By reviewing the management of previous projects

B By defining the customer's expectations of the project's products

C By defining cost tolerances for project objectives

D By delegating responsibilities to a different level of management

The correct answer is A. This should be deduced from your knowledge that the 'learn from experience' principle requires PRINCE2 project teams to do this, so that lessons are sought, recorded and acted upon throughout the life of the project (3.2).

2.2.2 Examples of missing-word multiple choice questions

Identify the missing word(s) in the following sentence

The reasons for undertaking the project must drive the [?] *and should be used to continually align the project progress to the business objectives.*

A Delivery strategy

B Decision making

C Benefits management approach

D Tolerances

The answer is B. The purpose of the business case theme is to establish mechanisms to judge whether the project is (and remains) desirable, viable and achievable as a means to support decision-making in its (continued) investment and reinforcing the principle of continued business justification (6.1).

Identify the missing word in the following sentence

A purpose of the [?] *theme is to control any unacceptable deviations from the project's objectives.*

A Change

B Plans

C Progress

D Risk

The answer is C. The purpose of the progress theme is to control any unacceptable deviations from the project's objectives (12.1).

2.2.3 Examples of list (two correct items) multiple choice questions

Which statements apply to a stage plan?

1. It is produced for the project during the 'initiating a project' process
2. It is produced close to the time when the planned events will take place
3. It provides the basis for day-to-day control by the project manager
4. It provides the basis for control by the project board

   A 1 and 2

   B 2 and 3

   C 3 and 4

   D 1 and 4

Answer is B. Statement 2 is correct because a stage plan is created towards the end of the preceding stage as part of the 'managing a stage boundary' process. It is produced close to the time when the planned events will take place (9.2.1.2). Statement 3 is also correct because a stage plan is created at the level of detail needed to enable the day-to-day control by the project manager (9.2.1.2).

Which roles CANNOT be combined with the role of project assurance?

1. Project manager
2. Project support
3. Senior user
4. Executive

   A 1 and 2

   B 2 and 3

   C 3 and 4

   D 1 and 4

Answer is A. As project assurance must be independent of the project manager and project support and is the responsibility of the project board (7.2.1.10, 7.2.1.2, 7.2.1.3, Tables 6.1, 7.1).

2.2.4 Example of negative multiple choice questions

Which role should NOT be combined with the role of project manager?

A Executive

B Senior supplier

C Project assurance

D Team manager

Answer is A. The executive and project manager roles cannot be combined (7.2.1.10).

2.3 Foundation exam structure

The foundation paper covers the four learning outcomes set out in Table 2.2. The scoring is explained in Table 2.3. Candidates taking the exam in a language that is not their native or working language may be awarded 25% extra time (i.e. 75 minutes in total). Other special considerations are available (e.g. for those with disabilities) and evidence should be supplied when booking the exam to ensure that requirements are adequately catered for.

Table 2.2 Foundation exam structure and weighting

Learning outcome		No. of questions	Weighting
1	Understand key concepts relating to projects and PRINCE2	5	8%
2	Understand how the PRINCE2 principles underpin the PRINCE2 method	8	13%
3	Understand the PRINCE2 themes and how they are applied throughout the project	31	52%
4	Understand the PRINCE2 processes and how they are carried out throughout the project	16	27%
Total number of marks		60	100%

Table 2.3 Foundation scoring

Number of questions	60
Time	60 minutes
Marks	Each question is worth 1 mark; 60 marks are available. There is no negative marking
Pass mark	55% or higher – a raw score of 33 marks or above

Note: unlike the PRINCE2 foundation exam for the 5th edition, there are no longer any trial questions in the exam.

2.4 Foundation hints and tips

2.4.1 Approach

Here are two alternative approaches to taking your exam. You should choose the approach that suits you best.

2.4.1.1 Approach A

Step 1

Go through the paper in a first non-stop 'sweep', answering all the straightforward questions to which you are certain you know the answers; ignore any long questions or those which will take longer to work out. When you have completed the first sweep you should have most of the questions answered.

If you are doing a paper-based exam, please complete the answer sheet with your selected answers as you progress through the exam paper. Do not leave it until the end and run out of time! Clearly mark any questions that you need to return to so that you do not miss them. Do not make notes on the answer sheet.

If you are doing the exam online, you can either complete an answer before you move to the next question or leave it and return to it at a later time. In addition, you can 'flag' or mark up a question for you to return to and review later. Take a look at the screen layout in Appendix A (Figure A.1) to see what this will look like.

Step 2

Return to the more difficult questions in a second sweep. Many will not be as tricky as they first appeared and, with a bit of common sense and careful reading of the question, you should be able to discount many of the options presented. This may leave you with one option which, on reflection, is clearly the correct one.

For other questions, you may be left with, say, two options from which you still cannot choose. Make sure that you re-read the question, focusing on key words, and make your selection. If you think you will have time, you may be able to leave these and continue the second sweep. You should feel confident that you are well beyond the pass mark and still have time to spare. However, it may be better to put a 'best guess' down now rather than leave it until later in case you do not have time to return to the question.

Step 3

If you have any questions left and you still have time, you can return for a third sweep. Review the question and the remaining options. For some questions, the answer may now suggest itself. For others, think about them again, but before time runs out, make a guess. You should have at least a 50:50 chance of being right.

If you don't have the time to do a third sweep, do make sure you have an answer against every question.

2.4.1.2 Approach B

You may prefer to follow this alternative approach if you are finding it difficult to complete the sample papers in the time allowed.

Step 1

Select an answer for every question on your first sweep through the paper, even if it is more of a guess. This way you at least have an answer even if it is a 'best guess'.

Step 2

If you have time, come back and review the questions where you made a guess at the end of the exam.

2.4.1.3 Note

Beware of changing answers you have already selected – experience indicates that there are probably as many changes made from correct to incorrect answers as there are from incorrect to correct! If you do need to make a change on a paper-based exam, however, make sure you show it clearly by erasing your previous selection and making sure that your new answer is clearly darker than the original. For an online exam, simply select your revised answer.

As with any exam make sure you have read the question and are answering the question asked rather than a closely related question to which you know the answer. Remember that no support material is permitted as this is a closed-book exam.

2.4.2 Time management

The exam is 60 minutes in duration. Candidates must manage their time in order to complete all questions. All 60 questions should be attempted. This means that there is only 1 mark per minute. So, there isn't much time to waste. If you are not sure of an answer, make a guess and mark it up to return to later.

2.4.2.1 For paper-based exams

If you wish to write your answers on the question paper first, you must be aware of the additional time needed to complete the answer sheet. Only answers submitted on the answer sheet provided will contribute to the result. Therefore, it is strongly recommended that you complete the answer sheet as you go through the paper rather than leaving it until the end to complete.

2.4.2.2 For online exams

You will have been provided with a voucher code by the ATO. This will enable you to book a time slot for your examination with PeopleCert. You will be required to download some software in preparation for the exam start. Detailed instructions will be supplied by PeopleCert once you have booked your time slot. You will need a quiet room to sit the exam and a device with a webcam. The room will need to be clear of anything that could assist you in taking the exam.

Please take a look at the screen layout in Appendix A (Figure A.1). Pay particular attention to:

- Where the 'next' and 'previous' buttons are
- How to flag questions to return to them later if you want to review them
- The location of the countdown timer so you can check how much time you have left
- How you can tell how many questions have been completed and how many you have left to answer.

Further information on taking your exam online is included in Appendix A.

2.4.2.3 Paper-based exams only using the mark sheet

If you are doing a paper-based exam, the answer sheet will need to be read electronically and the results generated by computer. It is therefore essential that candidates follow the instructions. The oval must be filled in using a pencil, not a pen. If a pen is used, the answers will not be marked.

Acceptable ways to complete the answer sheet are either by completely filling in the oval (at least 80% filled). Any other method, including ticks or crosses, is not acceptable and will not be marked (see Figure 2.1).

If a candidate wishes to change their answer during the exam, the incorrect answer should be erased completely and the revised answer clearly indicated. If more than one answer is given by the candidate, the question will score zero, as only one answer is required.

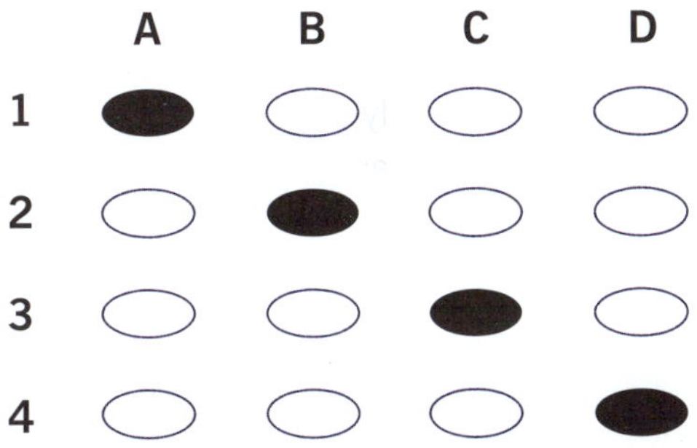

Figure 2.1 Acceptable ways to complete the answer sheet

2.5 Foundation exam sample paper

Question booklet: multiple choice

Exam duration: 1 hour

Instructions

1 You should attempt all 60 questions. Each question is worth one mark.

2 There is only one correct answer per question.

3 You need to answer 33 questions correctly to pass the exam.

4 Mark your answers on the answer sheet provided. Use a pencil (NOT pen).

5 You have 1 hour to complete this exam.

6 This is a 'closed-book' exam. No material other than the exam paper is allowed.

Questions

1. Which statement about controls is CORRECT?

A A highlight report is an event-driven control

B An exception report is a time-driven control

C A daily log is an event-driven control

D A checkpoint report is a time-driven control

2. Which document is used to identify interested parties that need to be informed of project closure?

A Change control approach

B End project report

C Communication management approach

D Project brief

3. Identify the missing words in the following sentence.

Any change to the products agreed at the start of a stage is monitored as part of the [?] *process, on a day-to-day basis.*

A Directing a project

B Controlling a stage

C Managing a stage boundary

D Closing a project

4. Which two statements about the 'continued business justification' principle are CORRECT?

   1 The business justification for a project should be documented
   2 The project manager should be responsible for the business justification
   3 A project must be stopped if the business justification changes
   4 Compulsory projects still require business justification

   A 1 and 2
   B 2 and 3
   C 3 and 4
   D 1 and 4

5. PRINCE2 mandates that the project board represents the primary stakeholder interests. Which principle does this follow?

   A Manage by stages
   B Focus on products
   C Defined roles and responsibilities
   D Learn from experience

6. When is it confirmed whether a project's objectives have been achieved?

   A During the 'closing a project' process
   B During the final end stage assessment
   C During the 'controlling a stage' process
   D During the 'managing product delivery' process

7. Which statement correctly describes project assurance and quality assurance?

   A Project assurance provides assurance to the project's stakeholders whereas quality assurance provides assurance to the wider corporate, programme or customer organization
   B They are both the responsibility of the project board, but project assurance may be delegated
   C They are both independent of the project management team
   D Project assurance and quality assurance are both the responsibility of corporate, programme management or the customer

8. Identify the missing words in the following sentence.

   If a baselined product requires modification, the recommended [?] *procedure, or equivalent procedure should be used.*

A Risk management

B Exception management

C Issue and change control

D Quality control

9. According to the 'manage by exception' principle, what should be defined to establish limits of delegated authority?

A Scope of the project

B Costs of the project

C Timescales for the project

D Tolerances for the project

10. Which two statements are CORRECT about the minimum requirements for applying the change theme?

1 Identified issues must be assessed for their impact on the business justification for the project.

2 Project issues must be captured, examined and managed throughout the project lifecycle.

3 The actual status of products must be verified to ensure that this matches the authorized state.

4 A budget must be established to pay for requests for change and their analysis.

A 1 and 2

B 2 and 3

C 3 and 4

D 1 and 4

11. Which is a purpose of the 'controlling a stage' process?

A To agree, perform and deliver project work

B To draft a plan for the next stage

C To agree tolerances for the stage

D To take action so that the stage remains within tolerance

12. What is likely to be avoided by applying the 'tailor to suit the project' principle?

A Unnecessary management effort

B Project risks

C Training

D Procurement procedures

13. Which is a responsibility of the team manager role?
    - A To accept authorized work packages from the project manager
    - B To review the highlight report for the previous reporting period
    - C To review the tailoring approach and its implications for project controls
    - D To examine and escalate issues, taking necessary corrective actions

14. In which situation might the 'controlling a stage' process be used?
    - A To manage a long initiation stage of a complex project
    - B To manage the activities of a complex programme
    - C To organize support activities following the handover of products to operations
    - D To create an exception plan to replace the current stage plan

15. Which is a step in PRINCE2's recommended approach to planning?
    - A Identify activities and dependencies
    - B Describe the means of communication for the project
    - C Implement responses for opportunities
    - D Baseline the project deliverables

16. What is an advantage of applying the 'learn from experience' principle?
    - A It allows the project board to delegate cost tolerances to the project manager
    - B It allows the project team to fully understand their roles and responsibilities
    - C It allows the project manager to delegate time tolerances to the team managers
    - D It allows the project team to identify improvements to be made during the project

17. Which is a responsibility of the business representative on the project board?
    - A To set tolerance levels for the project
    - B To ensure the project represents value for money
    - C To confirm the project delivers the required functionality
    - D To check the required quality levels are achieved by the project's products

18. What makes a project a PRINCE2 project?
    - A It has project processes that satisfy the objectives of PRINCE2 processes
    - B It has a permanent project organization to deliver a long-term result
    - C It has established technology to improve business as usual
    - D It applies some of the PRINCE2 principles

19. What is risk probability?
    - A The scale of the risk should it occur
    - B The probable effect on the project being able to deliver its objectives
    - C A probable timeframe within which the risk may occur
    - D A measure of the likelihood of the risk occurring

20. Which describes the 'implement' step within the recommended risk management procedure?
    - A Project support allocates the risk budget to fund the selected risk responses
    - B The risk owner decides the best response to control the risk
    - C The risk owner and the risk actionee carry out activities to control and deal with the risk
    - D The project manager formulates the risk management approach

21. Which is an objective of the 'initiating a project' process?
    - A To ensure that there is authority to initiate the project
    - B To prepare the plans for the subsequent delivery stages
    - C To summarize how the organization's project management method will be tailored for the project
    - D To request authority from programme, corporate management or the customer to deliver the project

22. Which is a minimum requirement for applying the risk theme?
    - A To assign risk actionees to undertake planned risk responses
    - B To escalate identified threats to the project board
    - C To record identified threats in a risk register
    - D To establish a risk budget to fund responses to risks

23. If a work package is forecast to exceed its tolerances, how should a team manager inform the project manager?
    - A By submitting an exception report
    - B By submitting an exception plan
    - C By raising an issue
    - D By raising a risk

45. Which is a purpose of a quality management approach?

A To define the customer's quality expectations for the project

B To define the quality standards to be applied to a project

C To identify the level of quality required for each of the project's products

D To summarize the planned quality management activities

46. How does defining a product's quality requirements support the 'focus on products' principle?

A By providing the project's tolerances so that authority can be delegated

B By providing the responsibilities for the project management team

C By providing the justification for the project to be initiated

D By providing an explicit understanding of what the project must deliver

47. Which is a feature of PRINCE2?

A It is a method specifically designed for technical projects

B It promotes continual learning in organizations

C It includes many motivational techniques

D It is designed to manage both projects and programmes

48. Which roles should NOT be combined?

A Project board and change authority

B Project manager and team manager

C Executive and project manager

D Project manager and project support

49. Which is a characteristic of a project?

A It is considered low risk

B It avoids stresses and strains between organizations

C It maintains business as usual

D It involves cross-functional teams

50. Which is an objective of the 'managing a stage boundary' process?

A To request authorization to start the next stage

B To ensure that all threats and opportunities for the current stage have been closed

C To ensure that work on products allocated to the team for the next stage is authorized

D To implement actions to resolve tolerance deviations from the stage plan

51. In which process is authorization given to deliver the project's products?

- **A** Starting up a project
- **B** Initiating a project
- **C** Managing a stage boundary
- **D** Directing a project

52. Which is a minimum requirement for applying the business case theme?

- **A** To document the responsibility for defining the standards for the business case
- **B** To appoint a senior user from an area of the business impacted by the project
- **C** To have the benefits management approach approved by the participants of benefits reviews
- **D** To delegate the development of the business justification to the project manager

53. How is the project initiation documentation used during the 'closing a project' process?

- **A** It is used as the basis for comparing the original aim of the project against what was actually achieved
- **B** It provides the controls for the final stage of the project
- **C** It is updated to include relevant lessons from previous projects
- **D** It provides the project product description for approval by the project board

54. Which process aims to ensure that during the project all parties understand the project objectives?

- **A** Starting up a project
- **B** Directing a project
- **C** Initiating a project
- **D** Managing product delivery

55. When should the 'managing a stage boundary' process be undertaken?

- **A** Close to the end of each management stage
- **B** Close to the start of each management stage
- **C** At the end of the final stage
- **D** At the end of the 'starting up a project' process

56. What is a project outcome?

A A measurable improvement that is perceived as an advantage by one or more stakeholders

B The reason for the project

C The result of the change derived from using the project's outputs

D The project's specialist products

57. Identify the missing words in the following sentence.

The six aspects of project performance to be managed are [?], *costs, timescales and scope.*

A Benefits, change, risk

B Benefits, quality, risk

C Change, quality, risk

D Benefits, change, quality

58. Which management stages must a PRINCE2 project consist of, as a minimum?

A Starting up, initiation, and at least one other stage for the rest of the project

B At least one stage for developing products, and a closing stage

C Initiation, and at least one other stage for the rest of the project

D Initiation, at least one stage for developing products, and a closing stage

59. Which statement about project stakeholders is CORRECT?

A All stakeholders must be identified at the start of the project

B All stakeholders are members of the project board

C All stakeholders are external to the corporate organization

D All three principle categories of stakeholder have their interests represented by the project board

60. What should be provided by a project mandate?

A Terms of reference for a project

B A detailed business case

C Tolerances for each management stage

D A plan for the initiation stage

2.6 Foundation exam sample paper answers and rationales

Q	A	Syllabus ref	Rationale
1	D	3.7.3a	A. Incorrect. A highlight report is a time-driven control, produced at a predefined frequency. Ref 12.2.2 B. Incorrect. An exception report is an event-driven control, produced when a tolerance is forecast to be exceeded. Ref 12.2.2 C. Incorrect. A daily log is a useful tool for recording actions when reviewing progress, but it is not defined as a PRINCE2 control. Ref 12.2.2, A.7.1 D. **Correct**. A team manager prepares a checkpoint report for the project manager at a predefined frequency. Therefore, checkpoint reports are a time-driven control. Ref 12.2.2
2	C	3.2.1b	A. Incorrect. A change control approach is used to identify how, and by whom, the project's products will be controlled and protected. Ref A.3.1 B. Incorrect. An end project report is used during project closure to review how the project performed against the version of the project initiation documentation (PID) used to authorize it. Ref A.8.1 C. **Correct**. A communication management approach contains a description of the means and frequency of communication to parties both internal and external to the project. Ref A.5.1 D. Incorrect. A project brief is used to provide a full and firm foundation for the initiation of the project and is created in the 'starting up a project' process. It is not used in the 'closing a project' process. Ref A.19.1
3	B	4.2d	A. Incorrect. The purpose of the 'directing a project' process is to enable the project board to be accountable for the project's success by making key decisions and exercising overall control while delegating day-to-day management of the project to the project manager. Ref 15.1 B. **Correct**. An objective of the 'controlling a stage' process is to ensure attention is focused on delivery of the stage's products. Any movement away from the direction and products agreed at the start of the stage is monitored to avoid uncontrolled change and loss of focus. The 'controlling a stage' process describes the work of the project manager in handling the day-to-day management of the stage. Ref 17.2, 17.3 C. Incorrect. The purpose of the 'managing a stage boundary' process is to enable the project manager to provide the project board with sufficient information to be able to confirm continued business justification and acceptability of the risks. Ref 19.1 D. Incorrect. The purpose of the 'closing a project' process is to provide a fixed point at which acceptance for the project product is confirmed, and to recognize that objectives set out in the original project initiation documentation (PID) have been achieved. Ref 20.1

Q	A	Syllabus ref	Rationale
4	D	2.1a	D. **Correct**. (1) Correct. PRINCE2 requires that, for all projects, the business justification is recorded and approved. Ref 3.1 (2) Incorrect. The business justification is the responsibility of the executive, not the project manager. Ref 6.2.1 (3) Incorrect. A project should be stopped if the justification disappears. However even though the justification should remain valid, it may still change. It is important for the evolving justification to be valid. Ref 3.1 (4) Correct. Even compulsory projects should be supported by a business justification that demonstrates value for money. Ref 3.1
5	C	2.1c	A. Incorrect. Application of the 'manage by stages' principle ensures that a PRINCE2 project is planned, monitored and controlled on a stage-by-stage basis. Ref 3.4 B. Incorrect. Application of the 'focus on products' principle ensures that a PRINCE2 project focuses on the definition and delivery of products, in particular their quality requirements. This principle does not represent the primary stakeholders. Ref 3.6 C. **Correct**. Application of the 'defined roles and responsibilities' principle ensures that a PRINCE2 project has defined and agreed roles and responsibilities within an organization structure that engages the business, user and supplier stakeholder interests. Ref 3.3 D. Incorrect. Application of the 'learn from experience' principle ensures that PRINCE2 project teams learn from previous experience: lessons are sought, recorded and acted upon throughout the life of the project. Ref 3.2
6	A	4.1g	A. **Correct**. The purpose of the 'closing a project' process is to provide a fixed point at which acceptance of the project product is confirmed, and to recognize that objectives set out in the original project initiation documentation have been achieved, or that the project has nothing more to contribute. Ref 20.1 B. Incorrect. There is not an end stage assessment at the end of the final stage. A purpose of the 'closing a project' process is to recognize that objectives set out in the original project initiation documentation have been achieved. Ref 20.1, 12.2.2.4 C. Incorrect. The 'controlling a stage' process describes the work of the project manager in handling the day-to-day management of the stage. The achievement of a project's objectives is measured and confirmed during the 'closing a project' process. Ref 17.3, 20.1 D. Incorrect. The 'managing product delivery' process is used to control delivery of the project's products at work package level and interfaces with the 'controlling a stage' process. A purpose of the 'closing a project' process is to recognize that objectives set out in the original project initiation documentation have been achieved. Ref 20.1, 18.2

Table continues

Answers and rationales *continued*

Q	A	Syllabus ref	Rationale
7	A	3.3.3b	A. **Correct**. Quality assurance provides assurance to corporate, programme management or customer on the project's compliance with relevant corporate, programme management or customer standards and policies. Project assurance provides assurance to the project's stakeholders that the project is being conducted properly. Ref Tab. 8.1, 8.1.1 B. Incorrect. Quality assurance is the responsibility of the programme or corporate organization. Ref Tab. 8.1, 8.1.1 C. Incorrect. Quality assurance is independent of the project. Project assurance is independent of the project manager, but not the project. Ref Tab. 8.1, 8.1.1 D. Incorrect. Project assurance is the responsibility of the project board. Quality assurance is the responsibility of corporate, programme management or customer. Ref Tab. 8.1, 8.1.1
8	C	3.6.3b	A. Incorrect. This procedure assesses and controls uncertainty, not change. Ref 10.4 B. Incorrect. When there is an exception situation, this must be raised to the next level of management. This is part of the progress theme rather than a defined procedure. Ref 12.2.3 C. **Correct**. This procedure identifies and controls changes to baselined products. The PRINCE2 recommended issue and change control procedure can be used, or an equivalent procedure. Ref 11.4.1–4 D. Incorrect. This activity defines and implements methods to check that products will meet their quality criteria. Ref 8.1.1
9	D	2.1e	A. Incorrect. Project scope must be defined, but it is the tolerances that define limits of delegated authority. Ref 3.5 B. Incorrect. Project cost must be defined, but it is the tolerances that define limits of delegated authority. Ref 3.5 C. Incorrect. Timescales must be defined, but it is the tolerances that define limits of delegated authority. Ref 3.5 D. **Correct**. A PRINCE2 project has defined tolerances for each project objective to establish limits of delegated authority. Ref 3.5
10	A	3.6.2	A. **Correct**. (1) Correct. To be following PRINCE2, a project must, as a minimum, assess whether identified issues might have a material impact on the business justification of the project (PRINCE2's 'continued business justification' principle). Ref 11.2 (2) Correct. To be following PRINCE2, a project must, as a minimum, ensure that project issues are captured, examined, managed and reviewed throughout the project lifecycle. Ref 11.2 (3) Incorrect. As part of the change theme, verification of the actual status of products can be considered, however this is not a minimum requirement. Ref. 11.2, 11.3.3 (4) Incorrect. Unless the anticipated level of change on a project is low, it is advisable for a budget to be set up to pay for changes. However, this is not a minimum requirement for applying the change theme. Ref 11.2, 11.3.6

Q	A	Syllabus ref	Rationale
11	D	4.1d	A. Incorrect. To agree, perform and deliver project work is a purpose of the 'managing product delivery' process. Ref 18.1 B. Incorrect. To draft a plan for the next stage is a purpose of the 'managing a stage boundary' process. Ref 19.1 C. Incorrect. The stage plan for the next stage is created in the 'managing a stage boundary' process and approved in the 'directing a project' process. During the 'authorize a stage or exception plan activity', tolerances will be set for the stage plan being approved. Ref 19.1, 15.4.3 D. **Correct**. The purpose of the 'controlling a stage' process is to assign work, monitor it, deal with issues, report progress and take corrective action to ensure that the stage remains within tolerance. Ref 17.1
12	A	2.1g	A. **Correct**. If PRINCE2 is not tailored, it is unlikely that the project management effort and approach would be appropriate for the needs of the project. Tailoring ensures the project management method used is appropriate to the project's environment. Ref 3.7 B. Incorrect. Tailoring is done according to the project's risk. It does not avoid risk. Ref 3.7 C. Incorrect. Tailoring does not avoid the need for training. It does ensure that the project management method and controls are appropriate to the project's environment. Training may still be necessary. Ref 3.7 D. Incorrect. Tailoring will align the project method to the business processes that may govern and support the project, such as human resources, finance and procurement. It does not avoid the need for these processes. Ref 3.7
13	A	3.2.3h	A. **Correct**. The team manager's primary responsibility is to ensure production of those products allocated by the project manager. PRINCE2 uses work packages to allocate work to team managers. Ref 7.2.1.8 B. Incorrect. Reviewing the highlight report for the previous reporting period is a responsibility of the project manager in the 'controlling a stage' process. Ref 7.2.1.7, 17.4.5 C. Incorrect. Reviewing the tailoring approach and its implications for project controls is a responsibility of the project manager in the 'initiating a project' process. Ref 7.2.1.7, 16.4.6 D. Incorrect. Capturing, examining and escalating issues and risks, and taking corrective actions, are responsibilities of the project manager in the 'controlling a stage' process. Ref 7.2.1.7, 17.4
14	A	4.3d	A. **Correct**. For complex projects with a large initiation stage, the 'controlling a stage' process can be used to control the activities. Ref 17.3 B. Incorrect. The 'controlling a stage' process is used by the project manager to manage the day-to-day activities of a stage, not a programme. Ref 17.3 C. Incorrect. Support activities are business as usual. 'Controlling a stage' is a project process. Ref 17.3 D. Incorrect. Creating an exception plan is an activity within the 'managing a stage boundary' process. Ref 19.4.5

Table continues

Answers and rationales *continued*

Q	A	Syllabus ref	Rationale
15	A	3.4.3a	A. **Correct**. 'Identifying activities and dependencies' is a step in PRINCE2's recommended approach to planning. The step identifies the activities required to deliver a planned product. Ref Fig. 9.2, 9.3.1.3 B. Incorrect. Describing the means of communication in the project is done as part of creating the communication management approach. Ref 7.2.2 C. Incorrect. Implementing responses for risks is part of the recommended risk management process. Ref 10.3.2 D. Incorrect. The 'baselining project deliverables' activity takes place whenever a product is either ready for review or has been approved. Ref 11.1
16	D	2.1b	A. Incorrect. A PRINCE2 project has defined tolerances for each project objective to establish limits of delegated authority. This is an advantage of applying the 'manage by exception' principle. Ref 3.5 B. Incorrect. A PRINCE2 project has defined and agreed roles and responsibilities within an organization structure that engages the business, user and supplier stakeholder interests. This is an advantage of applying the 'defined roles and responsibilities' principle. Ref 3.3 C. Incorrect. A PRINCE2 project has defined tolerances for each project objective to establish limits of delegated authority. This is an advantage of applying the 'manage by exception' principle. Ref 3.5 D. **Correct**. As the project progresses the project should continue to learn. Lessons should be included in relevant reports and reviews. The goal is to seek opportunities to implement improvements during the life of the project. Ref 3.2
17	B	3.2.3b	A. Incorrect. Project tolerance levels are set by corporate or programme management. The project board sets stage tolerance levels. Ref 12.2.1 B. **Correct**. The executive (who represents the business interest) is appointed to ensure that the project is focused on achieving and delivering a product that will achieve the forecast benefits and will deliver value for money. Ref 7.2.1.2 C. Incorrect. Confirming the project delivers the required functionality is part of the responsibilities/focus of the senior user who is appointed by the executive. Ref 7.2.1.3, C.3.1 D. Incorrect. Checking the required quality levels are achieved by the project's products is part of the responsibilities/focus of the senior supplier who is appointed by the executive. Ref 7.2.1.4
18	A	1.1d	A. **Correct**. As one of the minimum requirements, a PRINCE2 project must demonstrate that the project has processes that satisfy the purpose and objectives of the PRINCE2 processes. Ref 1.3 B. Incorrect. A project organization is always temporary. For this reason having a permanent structure is not a minimum requirement. Ref 2.1 C. Incorrect. A project is a means to change an existing business as usual. However, PRINCE2 does not define how this change is going to take place. Technology to improve the business as usual will be an output for the project, and PRINCE2 will be tailored to manage the delivery of that output. Ref 2.1 D. Incorrect. Application of all of the PRINCE2 principles is mandatory. Ref 1.3

Q	A	Syllabus ref	Rationale
35	D	3.2.3f	A. Incorrect. It is a responsibility of project assurance to ensure an acceptable solution is being developed. Ref 7.2.1.5 B. Incorrect. It is a responsibility of the team manager to prepare a team plan and agree it with the project manager. Ref 7.2.1.8 C. Incorrect. It is a responsibility of project support to maintain project files according to document control procedures. Ref 7.2.1.9 D. **Correct**. It is the project board's responsibility to agree to each change before it's implemented. The project board may delegate some authority for approving or rejecting requests for change to the change authority. Ref 7.2.1.6
36	B	2.1d	A. Incorrect. The 'focus on products' principle ensures that the project focuses on the definition and delivery of products, in particular their quality requirements. Ref 3.6 B. **Correct**. The focus on managing by stages ensures that the project is properly initiated before work starts on delivery of the project's outputs. Ref 3.4 C. Incorrect. The 'defined roles and responsibilities' principle defines an organization structure that engages the business, user and supplier stakeholder interests, setting out who is accountable. Ref 3.3 D. Incorrect. The 'continued business justification' principle defines that a project must be desirable, viable and achievable. Ref 3.1
37	C	3.4.3c	A. Incorrect. The length of management stages can be longer when risk is lower – a complex risk is unlikely to be lower risk. Ref 9.3.1.1 B. Incorrect. The length of management stages can be longer when risk is lower – understanding risk does not make a risk lower. Ref 9.3.1.1 C. **Correct**. The length of management stages can be longer when risk is lower, typically in the middle of projects. Ref 9.3.1.1 D. Incorrect. The length of management stages can be shorter when risk is higher. Ref 9.3.1.1
38	B	4.3g	A. Incorrect. When handing over products, the benefits management approach is checked to ensure that post-project benefits reviews are planned. However, these are performed after the project, not within the 'closing a project process'. Ref 20.4.3 B. **Correct**. During the 'closing a project' process, ownership of the products is transferred to the customer and the responsibility of the project management team is then terminated. Ref 20.3, 20.4.3 C. Incorrect. At the end of the final stage an end project report is created. Ref 20.4.4 D. Incorrect. The project closure notification is sent to the project board for review and approval in the 'directing a project' process. Ref 20.4.5, 15.4.5

Table continues

Answers and rationales *continued*

Q	A	Syllabus ref	Rationale
39	C	4.1a	A. Incorrect. To understand the resources and costs to deliver the project's products is an objective of the 'initiating a project' process. Ref 16.1 B. Incorrect. To ensure that there is authority to deliver the project's products is an objective of the 'directing a project' process. Ref 15.1 C. **Correct**. The 'starting up a project' process is a lighter process compared to the more detailed and thorough 'initiating a project' process. Ref 14.1 D. Incorrect. The suite of management products make up the project initiation documentation which is created during the 'initiating a project' process. Ref 16.3
40	C	1.2b	A. Incorrect. PRINCE2 refers to the organization that commissions a project as 'corporate, programme management or the customer'. This organization is responsible for providing the project's mandate, governing the project, and for realizing any benefits that the project might deliver. Ref 2.5 B. Incorrect. PRINCE2 refers to the organization that commissions a project as 'corporate, programme management or the customer'. This organization is responsible for providing the project's mandate. Ref 2.5 C. **Correct**. PRINCE2 refers to a supplier as the person, group or groups responsible for the supply of the project's specialist products. Ref 2.5 D. Incorrect. The senior user provides the customer's quality expectations and defines acceptance criteria for the project. The senior user will define and verify user requirements and expectations. Ref C.3.1, Tab. 7.1
41	C	3.2.2	A. Incorrect. It is the responsibility of the senior user to verify user requirements, but it is not a minimum requirement. Ref 7.2, Tab. 7.1 B. Incorrect. A delegated change authority is optional, not a minimum requirement. Ref 7.2 C. **Correct**. To be following PRINCE2, a project must, as a minimum, define its organization structure and roles. This must minimally ensure that all of the responsibilities in PRINCE2's role descriptions are fulfilled. Ref 7.2 D. Incorrect. It is the responsibility of the senior supplier to provide supplier resources, but it is not a minimum requirement to ensure they are available. Ref 7.2, Tab. 7.1
42	B	4.2e	A. Incorrect. When a work package is being negotiated is when the project manager and team manager agree the timing of checkpoint reports. Ref 12.2.2.4, 18.4.1 B. **Correct**. A team manager is required to provide checkpoint reports at the frequency agreed with the project manager in the relevant work package. Ref 18.2, 12.2.2.4, 18.4.2 C. Incorrect. Checkpoints are a time-driven control and done at a frequency agreed in the work package, not driven by such events as completing quality-checking activities. Ref 12.2.2.4, 18.4.2 D. Incorrect. The team manager is not involved in reviewing how a stage is progressing. Ref 12.2.2.2, 17.4.4, Tab. 17.4

Q	A	Syllabus ref	Rationale
43	A	4.1b	A. **Correct**. The 'directing a project' process provides a mechanism for the project board to achieve such assurance without being overburdened by project activity. Ref 15.3 B. Incorrect. The 'directing a project' process covers the activities of those at the level of management above the project manager. Ref 15.3 C. Incorrect. The project board manage by exception. It monitors via reports and controls through a small number of decision points. There should be no need for other 'progress meetings' for the project board. Ref 15.3 D. Incorrect. The 'directing a project' process starts on completion of the 'starting up a project' process. Ref 15.1
44	C	3.4.1a	A. Incorrect. The purpose of the risk theme is to identify, assess and control uncertainty within the project. Ref 10.1 B. Incorrect. The identification of project products involves configuration management, part of the change theme. Ref 11.3.3 C. **Correct**. The purpose of the plans theme is to define the means of delivering the products. Ref 9.1 D. Incorrect. A benefits management approach is associated with the business case theme, not the plans theme. Ref 6.2, A.1.1
45	B	3.3.1b	A. Incorrect. The customer's quality requirements are defined in a project product description. Ref A.21.1 B. **Correct**. The quality management approach is used to define the quality techniques and standards to be applied during a project. Ref A.22.1 C. Incorrect. The level of quality required for each of a project's products is the quality specification that is recorded as the quality criteria in the associated product description. Ref A.17.1 D. Incorrect. The quality register is used to summarize all of the quality management activities that are planned. Ref A.23.1
46	D	2.1f	A. Incorrect. A product's quality criteria describe the criteria against which a product will be approved. The setting of tolerances supports the 'manage by exception' principle. Ref 3.5, A.17.5 B. Incorrect. A product's quality criteria describe the criteria against which a product will be approved. The defining of responsibilities supports the 'defined roles and responsibilities' principle. Ref 3.3, A.17.5 C. Incorrect. A product's quality criteria describe the criteria against which a product will be approved. The justification of the project supports the 'continued business justification' principle. Ref 3.1, A.17.5 D. **Correct**. A PRINCE2 project uses product descriptions to provide such clarity by defining each product's purpose, composition, derivation, format, quality criteria and quality method. Ref 3.6

Table continues

Answers and rationales *continued*

Q	A	Syllabus ref	Rationale
47	B	1.2a	A. Incorrect. PRINCE2's strength is in its wide applicability – it is entirely generic. Consequently, industry-specific or type-specific activity is excluded. Specific techniques can readily be used alongside PRINCE2. Ref 1.2 B. **Correct**. PRINCE2 promotes learning from project experience and continual improvement in organizations. Ref 1 C. Incorrect. Leadership styles and motivational skill vary greatly from one project environment to another. Hence, to keep the generic nature of PRINCE2 intact, such styles and skills are excluded. Ref 1.2 D. Incorrect. PRINCE2 is intended to be used to manage only projects, not programmes. Ref 1
48	C	3.2.3j	A. Incorrect. It is the project board's responsibility to agree to each potential change before it is implemented. In a project where few changes are envisaged, it may be reasonable to leave this authority in the hands of the project board. Ref 7.2.1.6 B. Incorrect. The team manager role may be assigned to the project manager or a separate person. Ref 7.2.1.8 C. **Correct**. The executive and project manager roles cannot be combined. The executive's accountability for project success cannot be delegated. Ref 7.2.1.10 D. Incorrect. Project support is the responsibility of the project manager. The role defaults to the project manager if it is not otherwise allocated. Ref 7.2.1.9
49	D	1.1a	A. Incorrect. Projects introduce threats and opportunities over and above those typically encountered in the course of business as usual. Ref 2.1 B. Incorrect. Projects often cross the normal functional divisions within an organization and sometimes span entirely different organizations. This frequently causes stresses and strains. Ref 2.1 C. Incorrect. A project is a temporary organization that is created for the purpose of delivering one or more business products. There are a number of characteristics of project work that distinguishes it from business as usual. Ref 2.1 D. **Correct**. Projects involve a team of people with different skills working together to introduce a change that will impact others outside the team. Ref 2.1

Q	A	Syllabus ref	Rationale
50	A	4.2f	A. **Correct**. An objective of the 'managing a stage boundary' process is for the project manager to request authorization from the project board to start the next stage. Ref 19.2 B. Incorrect. Risks do not have to be closed at the end of a stage. During each of the activities within the 'managing a stage boundary' process, the issue register and risk register are updated as necessary. Ref 17.4, 17.4.1–8 C. Incorrect. Ensuring that work on products allocated to the team for the next stage is authorized is an objective of the 'managing product delivery' process, which ensures that work on products allocated to a team is authorized and agreed in a work package. Ref 18.2 D. Incorrect. An exception plan may be prepared during the 'managing a stage boundary' process to show how to recover from a tolerance deviation, but selecting and implementing actions to resolve the deviation would occur as part of the 'take corrective action' activity in the 'controlling a stage' process. Ref 17.4.8
51	D	4.2b	A. Incorrect. The 'starting up a project' process only requests authorization to initiate a project. Ref Fig. 14.1 B. Incorrect. The 'initiating a project' process only requests authorization to deliver a project; it is the 'directing a project' process that provides the authority. Ref 16.3, 15.2 C. Incorrect. The 'managing a stage boundary' process only requests authorization to start the next stage; it is the 'directing a project' process that provides the authority. Ref 19.2, 15.2 D. **Correct**. An objective of the 'directing a project' process is to ensure that there is authority to deliver the project's products. Ref 15.2
52	A	3.1.2	A. **Correct**. It is a minimum requirement that the roles and responsibilities for the business case and benefits management are defined and documented. Therefore this includes responsibility for defining any standards to which the business case needs to be developed. Ref 6.2, Tab. 6.1 B. Incorrect. It is usually advisable that the senior user comes from an area of the business impacted by the change, but it is not a minimum requirement. Ref 6.2.3, 6.2 C. Incorrect. If corporate, programme management or the customer are to manage or participate in the benefits reviews, the project board may need to seek their approval but it is not a minimum requirement to obtain such approval. Ref 6.2.3, 6.2 D. Incorrect. Development of the business justification may be delegated, for example to the project manager. However, this is not a minimum requirement. Ref 6.2.1, 14.4.4, 6.2

Table continues

Answers and rationales *continued*

Q	A	Syllabus ref	Rationale
53	A	4.1i	A. **Correct**. The project initiation documentation, baselined in the 'initiating a project' process, is used during the 'closing a project' process as the benchmark to review how the project actually performed against its planned targets and tolerances. Ref 20.2, 20.4.4 B. Incorrect. The controls for the final stage are contained in the stage plan rather than the project initiation documentation. Ref 19.4.1 C. Incorrect. The lessons log and lesson report are not part of the project initiation documentation. Ref A.20.2 D. Incorrect. The project product description, which first forms part of the project brief and is then incorporated into the project initiation documentation, is approved during the 'initiating a project' process and at the end of each stage. It is not approved as part of the 'closing a project' process. Ref Fig. 15.3, Tab. 15.3, A.19.2
54	C	4.3c	A. Incorrect. The 'starting up a project' process aims to ensure that there is a clear project mandate that provides the terms of reference for the project and should contain sufficient information to identify at least the prospective executive of the project board. Ref 14.3 B. Incorrect. The 'directing a project' process provides a mechanism for the project board to meet its responsibility for ensuring that there is continued business justification without being overburdened by project activity. Ref 15.3 C. **Correct**. It is the 'initiating a project' process that aims to ensure that all parties are clear on what the project is intended to achieve, why it is needed and how the outcome is to be achieved. Ref 16.3 D. Incorrect. The 'managing product delivery' process views the project from the team manager's perspective and aims to ensure that products are created and delivered by the team to the project. Ref 18.3
55	A	4.3f	A. **Correct**. The 'managing a stage boundary' process should be executed at, or close to the end of, each management stage. The process is used to enable the project board to receive sufficient information to review the current stage before starting the next. Ref 19.1 B. Incorrect. The activities to manage a stage boundary should be planned to take place at, or close to the end of, each management stage, not at the start. Ref 19.1 C. Incorrect. The activities to manage a stage boundary should be planned to take place at, or close to the end of, each management stage. However, the 'closing a project' process occurs at the end of the final management stage. Ref 19.1, Fig. 13.1 D. Incorrect. The 'starting up a project' process is not a management stage and therefore does not use the 'managing a stage boundary' process. The 'managing a stage boundary' process is not used at the end of the 'starting up a project' process. Ref 14.3, Fig. 13.1

Q	A	Syllabus ref	Rationale
56	C	3.1.3	A. Incorrect. A measurable improvement that is perceived as an advantage by one or more stakeholders is a project's benefit. Ref 6.1, Glossary B. Incorrect. The reason for the project is why the project is required not the result of a change derived from using the project's outputs. Ref 6.1, 6.2, 6.2.1 C. **Correct**. A project outcome is the result of a change derived from using the project's outputs. Ref 6.1 D. Incorrect. The specialist products are defined as the project's outputs. Ref 6.1, Glossary
57	B	1.1b	B. **Correct**. The six aspects of project performance to be managed are costs, timescales, scope, quality, risk and benefits. Ref 2.3 A, C, D – Incorrect. The six aspects of project performance to be managed are costs, timescales, scope, quality, risk and benefits. Change is a theme. Ref 2.3, 11.1
58	C	3.4.2	A. Incorrect. 'Starting up a project' is a PRINCE2 process, not a stage. A process is a structured set of activities designed to accomplish a specific objective. Ref 14.1, 13.1, Fig. 13.1 B. Incorrect. To be following PRINCE2, a project must, as a minimum, have an initiation stage and at least one further management stage. 'Closing a project' is a process, not a stage. Ref 9.2, Fig. 13.1 C. **Correct**. To be following PRINCE2, a project must, as a minimum, have an initiation stage and at least one further management stage. Ref 9.2 D. Incorrect. 'Closing a project' is a process, not a stage. Ref 20.1, Fig. 13.1
59	D	3.2.4b	A. Incorrect. It is important to review the communication management approach at each stage boundary, not just at the start of the project, to ensure that it includes all the key stakeholders. Ref 7.2.2 B. Incorrect. Project board members are stakeholders representing the three primary categories: business, user and supplier. Ref 7.1 C. Incorrect. Stakeholders may be internal or external to the corporate organization. Ref 7.1 D. **Correct**. The three principal categories of stakeholders: business, user and supplier, are represented by the executive, senior user(s) and senior supplier(s). Ref 7.1
60	A	4.3a	A. **Correct**. The project mandate should provide the terms of reference for a project. Ref 14.3 B. Incorrect. The detailed business case is produced during the 'initiating a project' process when the outline business case is updated. Ref 16.4.8 C. Incorrect. The project mandate may include the project tolerances but it is the project board's responsibility to identify stage tolerances. Ref 12.2.1 D. Incorrect. The creation of the plan for the initiation stage is the last activity during the 'starting up a project' process and is the responsibility of the project manager. Information from the project mandate may be contained in the plan but the actual plan itself is not included in the project mandate. Ref 14.4.6

3

Practitioner qualification

3 Practitioner qualification

Attaining the PRINCE2 foundation qualification is a prerequisite for undertaking the PRINCE2 practitioner examination, which assesses the ability of the candidate to apply their understanding of the PRINCE2 project management method to a given set of circumstances described in a scenario. Since 2014 AXELOS has also recognized the achievements of project management professionals who have attained relevant qualifications through other organizations (see the AXELOS website for a full list of other qualifying certifications for the PRINCE2 practitioner exam).

Typically, classroom training for PRINCE2 practitioners lasts one and a half days and the examination takes place at the end of the training (this will vary depending on training provider). However, as with foundation you can self-study for the practitioner exam and you may also choose to take the training in another format such as distance learning.

The target audience for this qualification is:

- project managers and aspiring project managers
- other key staff involved in the design, development and delivery of projects, including:
    - project board members (e.g. the executive sponsoring the project)
    - team managers (e.g. product delivery managers)
    - project assurance (including those from quality assurance or audit teams)
    - project support (e.g. project and programme office personnel)
    - operational line managers/staff (such as those who will be ensuring a smooth transition of the changes into business as usual and realizing the benefits).

3.1 Practitioner syllabus

Table 3.1 summarizes the practitioner syllabus, learning outcomes, assessment criteria, Bloom's levels and number of marks. The syllabus is available as a downloadable PDF at AXELOS.com.

Table 3.1 Practitioner examination: learning outcomes, assessment criteria, Bloom's levels and number of marks

Learning outcome		Assessment criteria*			BL	Marks
1	Apply the PRINCE2 principles in context	1.1	**Analyse** the application of PRINCE2 principles: a. Continued business justification (3.1) b. Learn from experience (3.2) c. Defined roles and responsibilities (3.3) d. Manage by stages (3.4) e. Manage by exception (3.5) f. Focus on products (3.6) g. Tailor to suit the project (3.7, 4.1, 4.3†), in context, through the integrated use of themes, processes and/or management products		4	8
2	Apply and tailor relevant aspects of PRINCE2 themes in context	2.1	**Business case theme**			
			2.1.1	**Apply** the PRINCE2 requirements for managing business justification (6.2†) a. Including the following management products: ● business case (A.2†) ● benefits management approach (A.1†) demonstrating an understanding of: b. Recommended roles and responsibilities within the theme (Tab. 6.1) c. Outputs, outcomes, benefits and dis-benefits (6.1, Fig. 6.1)	3	3
			2.1.2*	**Assess** whether an approach to managing business justification is effective and fit for purpose, taking into consideration: the context, the PRINCE2 principles, and the purpose and requirements of the business case theme (6–6.3†, 4.3†, 5.1, A.1†, A.2†, App. C†, 14.5.2, 16.5.2)	4	2

Table continues

Table 3.1 *continued*

Learning outcome		Assessment criteria*			BL	Marks
2	Apply and tailor relevant aspects of PRINCE2 themes in context *continued*	2.2	**Organization theme**			
			2.2.1	**Apply** the PRINCE2 requirements for managing organization (7.2†) a. Including the following management product: communication management approach (7.2.2, A.5†) demonstrating an understanding of: b. Recommended roles and responsibilities within the theme (Tab. 7.1) c. Recommended project management team structure (7.1–7.2†, Fig. 7.2, 7.3.1, 7.3.7, App. C†)	3	3
			2.2.2*	**Assess** whether an approach to managing organization is effective and fit for purpose, taking into consideration: the context, the PRINCE2 principles, and the purpose and requirements of the organization theme (7.1–7.2†, 7.3.1–7.3.5, 7.3.7, 4.3†, 5.1, 16.5.2, A.5†, App. C†, 15.5.2, 14/16/17/18/19/20.5.3)	4	2
		2.3	**Quality theme**			
			2.3.1	**Apply** the PRINCE2 requirements for managing quality (8.2) a. Including the following management products: • quality management approach (A.22†) • quality register (A.23†) • project product description (A.21†) • product description (A.17†) demonstrating an understanding of: b. Recommended roles and responsibilities within the theme (Tab. 8.1) c. The following activities: • quality planning (8.1.1, Fig. 8.1, 8.3.6, 8.3.8–8.3.9, 8.3.11) • quality control (8.1.1, Fig. 8.1) • quality assurance (8.1.1, 8.3.5)	3	3

Learning outcome	Assessment criteria*		BL	Marks
	2.3.2*	**Assess** whether an approach to managing quality is effective and fit for purpose, taking into consideration: the context, the PRINCE2 principles, and the purpose and requirements of the quality theme (Ch. 8† excl. 8.3.10 and 8.3.12, 4.3†, 5.1, 16.5.2, 19.5.2, A.17†, A.21–A.23†, App. C†)	4	2
2.4	**Plans theme**			
	2.4.1	**Apply** the PRINCE2 requirements for managing plans (9.2†) a. Including the following management products: ● project plan (9.2.1.1, A.16†) ● stage plan (9.2.1.2, A.16†) ● exception plan (9.2.1.3, A.16†) ● team plan (9.2.1.4, A.16†) demonstrating an understanding of: b. Recommended roles and responsibilities within the theme (Tab. 9.1) c. The recommended approach to planning, including the recommended product-based planning technique (9.3.1–9.3.7 excl. detailed estimating and resource scheduling techniques)	3	3
	2.4.2*	**Assess** whether an approach to managing plans is effective and fit for purpose, taking into consideration: the context, the PRINCE2 principles, and the purpose and requirements of the plans theme (9.1–9.3† excl. detailed estimating and resource scheduling techniques, 9.4.1, 4.3†, 5.1, 14.5.2, 16.5.2, 18.5.2, 19.5.2, A.16†, App. C†)	4	2

Table continues

Table 3.1 *continued*

Learning outcome		Assessment criteria*			BL	Marks
2	Apply and tailor relevant aspects of PRINCE2 themes in context *continued*	2.5	**Risk theme**			
			2.5.1	**Apply** the PRINCE2 requirements for managing risk (10.2) a. Including the following management products: ● risk management approach (A.24†) ● risk register (A.25†) demonstrating an understanding of: b. Recommended roles and responsibilities within the theme (Tab. 10.1) c. The recommended risk management procedure (10.3.2, 10.4† excl. risk estimation and evaluation techniques)	3	3
			2.5.2*	**Assess** whether an approach to risk is effective and fit for purpose, taking into consideration: the context, the PRINCE2 principles, and the purpose and requirements of the risk theme (Ch. 10† excl. risk estimation and evaluation techniques, 4.3†, 5.1†, 16.5.2, A.24–A.25†, App. C†)	4	2
		2.6	**Change theme**			
			2.6.1	**Apply** the PRINCE2 requirements for controlling change (11.2†) a. Including the following management products: ● change control approach (A.3†) ● configuration item record (A.6†) ● issue register (A.12†) ● issue report (A.13†) ● product status account (A.18†) demonstrating an understanding of: b. Recommended roles and responsibilities within the theme (Tab. 11.2) c. The recommended issue and change control procedure (11.4†, 11.3.6), including types of issue (11.1, Tab. 11.1)	3	3

Learning outcome	Assessment criteria*			BL	Marks
		2.6.2*	**Assess** whether an approach to controlling change is effective and fit for purpose, taking into consideration: the context, the PRINCE2 principles, and the purpose and requirements of the change theme (Ch. 11†, 4.3†, 5.1, 16.5.2, 17.5.2, A.3†, A.6†, A.12†, A.13†, A.18†, App. C†)	4	2
	2.7	**Progress theme**			
		2.7.1	**Apply** the PRINCE2 requirements for controlling progress (12.2†) a. Including the following management products: ● work package (A.26†) ● checkpoint report (A.4†) ● highlight report (A.11†) ● end stage report (A.9†) ● end project report (A.8†) ● exception report (A.10†) ● lessons log (A.14†) ● daily log (A.7†) demonstrating an understanding of: b. Recommended roles and responsibilities within the theme (Tab. 12.2) c. Tolerances and raising exceptions (12.2.1, 12.2.3)	3	3
		2.7.2*	**Assess** whether an approach to progress is effective and fit for purpose, taking into consideration: the context, the PRINCE2 principles, and the purpose and requirements of the progress theme (12.1–12.3†, 4.3†, 5.1, 14.5.2, 17.5.2, 18.5.2, 19.5.2, 20.5.2, A.4†, A.7–A.11†, A.14†, A.26†, App. C†)	4	2

Table continues

Chapter 3 – Practitioner qualification

Table 3.1 *continued*

Learning outcome		Assessment criteria*			BL	Marks
3	Apply and tailor relevant aspects of PRINCE2 processes in context	3.1	**Starting up a project process**			
			3.1.1	**Carry out** the starting up a project process activities (14.2–14.4†) and a. Recommended associated actions in each activity for: • appoint the executive and the project manager (14.4.1) • capture previous lessons (14.4.2) • design and appoint the project management team (14.4.3) • prepare the outline business case (14.4.4) • select the project approach and assemble the project brief (14.4.5, A.19†) • plan the initiation management stage (14.4.6) demonstrating an understanding of: b. Recommended roles and responsibilities within the process (Tabs 14.1–14.6) c. How the themes may be applied (Chs 6–12†)	3	3
			3.1.2*	**Assess** whether starting up a project process activities/actions, roles and responsibilities are effective and fit for purpose, taking into consideration: the context, the PRINCE2 principles, and the purpose and objectives of the process (Ch. 14† excl. 14.5.2, 4.3†, 13.4, A.19†, App. C†)	4	2
		3.2	**Directing a project process**			
			3.2.1	**Carry out** the directing a project process activities (15.2–15.4†) and a. Recommended associated actions: • authorize initiation (15.4.1) • authorize the project (15.4.2) • authorize a stage or exception plan (15.4.3) • give ad hoc direction (15.4.4) • authorize project closure (15.4.5) demonstrating an understanding of: b. Recommended roles and responsibilities within the process (Tabs 15.1–15.5) c. How the themes may be applied (Chs 6–12†)	3	3

Learning outcome	Assessment criteria*		BL	Marks
	3.2.2*	**Assess** whether directing a project process activities/actions, roles and responsibilities are effective and fit for purpose, taking into consideration: the context, the PRINCE2 principles, and the purpose and objectives of the process (Ch. 15†, 4.3†, 13.4, A.19†, App. C†)	4	2
3.3	**Initiating a project process**			
	3.3.1	**Carry out** the initiating a project process activities (16.2–16.4†) and a. Recommended associated actions: • agree the tailoring requirements (16.4.1) • prepare the risk management approach (16.4.2) • prepare the change control approach (16.4.3) • prepare the quality management approach (16.4.4) • prepare the communication management approach (16.4.5) • set up the project controls (16.4.6) • create the project plan (16.4.7) • refine the business case (16.4.8) • assemble the project initiation documentation (16.4.9, A.20†) demonstrating an understanding of: b. Recommended roles and responsibilities within the process (Tabs 16.1–16.9), and c. How the themes may be applied (Chs 6–12†)	3	3
	3.3.2*	**Assess** whether initiating a project process activities/actions, roles and responsibilities are effective and fit for purpose, taking into consideration: the context, the PRINCE2 principles, and the purpose and objectives of the process (Ch. 16† excl. 16.5.2, 4.3†, 13.4, A.20†, App. C†)	4	2

Table continues

Chapter 3 – Practitioner qualification

Table 3.1 *continued*

Learning outcome		Assessment criteria*			BL	Marks
3	Apply and tailor relevant aspects of PRINCE2 processes in context *continued*	3.4	**Controlling a stage process**			
			3.4.1	**Carry out** the controlling a stage process activities (17.2–17.4†) and a. Recommended associated actions: Work packages: ● authorize a work package (17.4.1) ● review work package status (17.4.2) ● receive completed work packages (17.4.3) Monitoring and reporting: ● review the management stage status (17.4.4) ● report highlights (17.4.5) Issues: ● capture and examine issues and risks (17.4.6) ● escalate issues and risks (17.4.7) ● take corrective action (17.4.8) demonstrating an understanding of: b. Recommended roles and responsibilities within the process (Tabs 17.1–17.8) c. How the themes may be applied (Chs 6–12†)	3	3
			3.4.2*	**Assess** whether controlling a stage process activities/actions, roles and responsibilities are effective and fit for purpose, taking into consideration: the context, the PRINCE2 principles, and the purpose and objectives of the process (Ch. 17† excl. 17.5.2, 4.3†, 13.4, App. C†)	4	2

Learning outcome	Assessment criteria*			BL	Marks
	3.5	Managing product delivery process			
		3.5.1	**Carry out** the managing product delivery process activities (18.2–18.4†) and a. Recommended associated actions: ● accept a work package (18.4.1) ● execute a work package (18.4.2) ● deliver a work package (18.4.3) demonstrating an understanding of: b. Recommended roles and responsibilities within the process (Tabs 18.1–18.3) c. How the themes may be applied (Chs 6–12†)	3	2
		3.5.2*	**Assess** whether managing product delivery process activities/actions, roles and responsibilities are effective and fit for purpose, taking into consideration: the context, the PRINCE2 principles, and the purpose and objectives of the process (Ch. 18† excl. 18.5.2, 4.3†, 13.4, App. C†)	4	2
	3.6	Managing a stage boundary process			
		3.6.1	**Carry out** the managing a stage boundary process activities (19.2–19.4†) and a. Recommended associated actions: ● plan the next management stage (19.4.1) ● update the project plan (19.4.2) ● update the business case (19.4.3) ● report management stage end (19.4.4) ● produce an exception plan (19.4.5) demonstrating an understanding of: b. Recommended roles and responsibilities within the process (Tabs 19.1–19.5) c. How the themes may be applied (Chs 6–12†)	3	2
		3.6.2*	**Assess** whether managing a stage boundary process activities/actions, roles and responsibilities are effective and fit for purpose, taking into consideration: the context, the PRINCE2 principles, and the purpose and objectives of the process (Ch. 19† excl. 19.5.2, 4.3†, 13.4, App. C†)	4	2

Table continues

Chapter 3 – Practitioner qualification

Table 3.1 *continued*

Learning outcome		Assessment criteria*			BL	Marks
3	Apply and tailor relevant aspects of PRINCE2 processes in context *continued*	3.7	**Closing a project process**			
			3.7.1	**Carry out** the closing a project process activities (20.2–20.4†) and a. Recommended associated actions: • prepare planned closure (20.4.1) • prepare premature closure (20.4.2) • hand over products (20.4.3) • evaluate the project (20.4.4) • recommend project closure (20.4.5) demonstrating an understanding of: b. Recommended roles and responsibilities within the process (Tabs 20.1–20.5) c. How the themes may be applied (Chs 6–12†)	3	2
			3.7.2*	**Assess** whether closing a project process activities/actions, roles and responsibilities and actions are effective and fit for purpose, taking into consideration: the context, the PRINCE2 principles, and the purpose and objectives of the process (Ch. 20† excl. 20.5.2, 4.3†, 13.4, App. C†)	4	2

* Primary references to the PRINCE2 manual are given in parentheses.

† Denotes inclusion of all subsections.

The verb (in bold type) for each syllabus area/assessment criterion indicates the Bloom's level: e.g. 'Apply', 'Carry out', indicates Level 3 Apply; 'Assess', 'Analyse' indicates Level 4 Analyse.

3.2 Practitioner exam based on a scenario

The practitioner exam is based on Bloom's Levels 3 and 4. As such you will be required to answer both application and analysis type questions. Therefore, you will need to read a one-page scenario. For paper-based exams this will be included in a separate scenario booklet. For online exams, you will find the button for the scenario at the top right-hand corner of your screen (see the screen layout shown in Appendix B).

An example of a scenario can be found in section 3.7. All examples of practitioner questions are based on this scenario.

Additional information

The **chief executive officer (CEO)** of the record company obtained finance from external investors to establish the company 10 years ago. He travels around the world to identify singers and groups to contract and then delegates their management to the vice president.

The **vice president** supervises the production of albums and associated products. Her annual bonus depends on the success of this project. She has no experience of using PRINCE2.

The **production manager**, who reports to the vice president, has successfully managed the delivery of several albums in the past, using a range of project management methods, including PRINCE2.

The **contracts manager** is a full-time employee of the record company and is responsible for ensuring that the contracts deliver the project. He is an experienced PRINCE2 project manager.

The **marketing director** is responsible, within the record company, for ensuring that marketing campaigns will deliver value for money.

The **marketing manager** has responsibility within the record company for delivering marketing campaigns that will achieve the required sales of albums and associated products.

The **production assistant** is employed by the record company to assist the production and marketing managers with documentation and communications.

The **singer's agent** is negotiating the contract between the singer and the record company. He will have an ongoing interest in the terms of the singer's contract.

The **singer** has not previously released an album. He has written a number of songs which may be recorded for this album.

The **music lawyer** is a specialist lawyer, contracted by the record company to ensure that the contracts, copyright, and project material are dealt with appropriately.

The **recording studio manager** is an employee of the recording studio contracted by the record company to produce the recordings. He is PRINCE2 qualified.

The **graphics designer** is employed by an external graphics design company. She will produce the artwork for the album.

The **events organizer** will plan the release event for the album which will include a live performance of the songs by the singer. He has a lot of experience of planning and monitoring small projects.

Questions

PRINCE2 principles

1. The chief executive officer (CEO) of the record company requires the cost-benefit analysis of every project to be recorded in a document called a 'project rationale'. The executive is preparing the draft 'project rationale' as part of the pre-project phase.

   Which principle is being applied, and why?

   A 'Continued business justification', because the justification for starting the project needs to be recorded in some form of a business case.

   B 'Continued business justification', because it is the executive who drafts the outline business case at the beginning of a project.

   C 'Learn from experience', because it is important to consider lessons from previous projects at the beginning of a new project.

   D 'Learn from experience', because the project management team should learn from more experienced corporate management.

2. During the initiation stage, the vice president stated that attendance at launch events held on Monday evenings is low, and on previous projects this had resulted in lower album sales. As a result, the launch event for this album will be held later in the week.

   Which principle is being applied, and why?

   A 'Continued business justification', because there is sufficient reason to start this project.

   B 'Continued business justification', because the project's justification should remain unchanged.

   C 'Learn from experience', because project teams should learn from what occurred on similar projects.

   D 'Learn from experience', because the project should continue to learn from its own experiences.

3. Towards the end of stage 2, the project manager realized that not all of the 'recorded sample songs' would be completed before the end of the stage. The project manager decided to move the remaining work to stage 3. This enabled the project manager to report that stage 2 was completed within time tolerance.

Is this an appropriate application of the 'manage by stages' principle, and why?

- A Yes, because moving the work to stage 3 avoided an exception situation in stage 2.
- B Yes, because stage 3 is not the final stage so work can be moved from stage 2.
- C No, because the project board should assess project viability on completion of work planned for stage 2.
- D No, because work in stage 3 should start while work planned for stage 2 is being completed.

4. The executive has appointed the company's finance manager to provide business assurance, to monitor whether the album sales will exceed the production costs as the project progresses through each stage.

How well does this apply the 'manage by exception' principle, and why?

- A It applies it well, because a PRINCE2 project should structure the project into management stages to enable approval on a stage-by-stage basis.
- B It applies it well, because the executive needs to be confident that controls and tolerances are being implemented effectively.
- C It applies it poorly, because roles should be combined in a small project as long as there is no conflict of interest.
- D It applies it poorly, because a PRINCE2 project should focus on delivering quality outputs rather than on the work required to deliver the products.

5. During the 'initiating a project' process, it was decided that the sound quality of the album should be the same, regardless of the delivery channel used. At the beginning of stage 4, the project manager agrees this requirement with the team manager responsible for delivering the album to the different channels.

Which principle is being applied, and why?

- A 'Manage by stages', because an output-oriented project should define the products prior to producing them.
- B 'Manage by stages', because users are more likely to be satisfied if the products are agreed at the start of the project.
- C 'Focus on products', because the work done will contribute to the products being delivered to the required standards.
- D 'Focus on products', because the project manager should make key decisions prior to the start of detailed work.

6. During stage 3, the music album project board consists of the vice president as the executive and senior user, with no senior supplier.

   Is this an appropriate application of the 'defined roles and responsibilities' principle, and why?

   A Yes, because the vice president can represent all three primary stakeholder interests.

   B Yes, because appointing the vice president provides an explicit project management team structure.

   C No, because the vice president cannot judge if the project can be feasibly delivered by all supply streams.

   D No, because having defined roles should help each person to answer 'what is expected of me?'

7. The work package to create the 'artwork' will commence in stage 3. The graphic design company uses their own development method to deliver products. They have appointed their graphic designer as the team manager to complete this work package. The project manager will review the appointment at the end of the stage.

   Which principle is being applied by the review, and why?

   A 'Manage by stages', because the project manager reviews the contents of the project initiation documentation when planning stage 4.

   B 'Manage by stages', because the project manager reviews the status of stage 3 products at the end of the stage.

   C 'Manage by exception', because the project board delegates the authority to the project manager on a stage-by-stage basis.

   D 'Manage by exception', because the team manager's performance should be reviewed before authorizing the next work package.

8. The project is in the initiation stage. The vice president requests that management products be produced in the form of slides, to be presented at project board meetings. This is in line with company policy.

   Is this an appropriate application of the 'tailor to suit the project' principle, and why?

   A Yes, because the controls applied need to be appropriate to the organization's governance.

   B Yes, because this provides control points during the project for decisions to be made.

C No, because producing slides takes more effort than producing written documents.

D No, because applying the 'manage by exception' principle removes the need for meetings.

PRINCE2 themes

Business case

Here are three actions related to managing business justification for the music album project.

Which role (A–F) should be responsible for each action?

Choose only one role for each action. Each role can be used once, more than once, or not at all.

9. Ensure that the law firm that is working on the contract between the singer and the record company will make a profit.

10. At a benefits review of the album launch, state whether the album sales met the targets specified in the business case.

11. Monitor monthly spend against the agreed budget on behalf of the record company.

A Executive.

B Senior user.

C Senior supplier.

D Project manager.

E Team manager.

F Project assurance.

12. The music album project is part of a programme to contract new singers. The 'artwork' is being produced by an external graphic designer. The graphic designer's profit has been documented in the record company's business case.

Is this appropriate, and why?

A Yes, because project costs should be recorded as part of the project's business case.

B Yes, because the project's business case should record any benefits for the project's stakeholder.

C No, because the project, as part of a programme, should be provided with the approach to the business case.

D No, because the graphic designer's business justification should not be part of the project's business case.

13. The project is in the initiation stage. When negotiating with the record company on behalf of the singer, the singer's agent stated that this type of music represents 3% of the total music market. The singer's agent understands the music industry and has been asked to specify how much profit the record company should expect to make from the sales of this album.

    Is this appropriate, and why?

    A Yes, because the agent has the skills required to be responsible for forecasting the album sales.

    B Yes, because the agent identified the size of the market for this type of music during the initiation stage.

    C No, because the senior user should be responsible for the development of the detailed business case.

    D No, because the senior user should be accountable for specifying the benefits which justify the project.

Organization

Use the 'Additional Information' in the scenario booklet to answer this question.

Here are three roles relating to the music album project.

Which individual (A–F) would be most appropriate for each role?

Choose only one individual for each role. Each individual can be used ONCE, or not at all.

14. Delegated user assurance.

15. Project manager.

16. Project support.

    A Vice president.

    B Production manager.

    C Production assistant.

    D Marketing manager.

    E Music lawyer.

    F Events organizer.

17. As a result of previous lessons, this recommendation has been made: 'If an executive is appointed who does not have an understanding of PRINCE2, someone with experience of applying PRINCE2 should undertake business assurance.' The recording studio manager has therefore been appointed as business assurance for stage 2.

    Is this appropriate, and why?

    A Yes, because the recording studio manager is responsible for the delivery of the 'recorded album'.

    B Yes, because the recording studio manager has the experience required to deliver the 'recorded album'.

    C No, because the recording studio manager's business justification may conflict with the interests of the executive.

    D No, because the recording studio manager will not be available throughout the project lifecycle.

18. The contracts manager has been appointed as the project manager for the music album project. In a previous job, the contracts manager worked as a graphic designer and, when planning for stage 3, decided to also take on the role of team manager for the 'artwork' production.

    Is this an appropriate application of the organization theme, and why?

    A Yes, because the project manager can take on a team manager role if they have the specialist skills.

    B Yes, because in a commercial environment the project manager should understand supplier contractual obligations.

    C No, because the team manager should come from the graphic design company to avoid conflicts of interest.

    D No, because the project manager should plan roles during the 'starting up a project' process.

Quality

Here are three items of information that will be included in the project product description for the 'album ready for launch'.

Under which heading (A–F) should they be recorded?

Choose only one heading for each item of information. Each heading can be used once, more than once, or not at all.

19. 'Recorded album', 'registered artwork' and 'launch event plan'.

20. The singer will give final approval of the 'artwork'.

21. The 'artwork' must comply completely with relevant equality legislation.

A Purpose.

B Composition.

C Development skills required.

D Project-level quality tolerances.

E Acceptance method.

F Acceptance responsibilities.

22. The record company must comply with music industry regulations when producing the 'artwork'.

Which action should the project manager take, and why?

A Record the need to meet this requirement during stage 2, because the 'artwork' will be delivered to the specified quality criteria during stage 3.

B Record the need to meet this requirement during stage 2, because the product description for the 'artwork' will specify the required quality criteria.

C Record the requirement in the quality management approach, because compliance with external standards should be addressed when determining the approach to quality.

D Record the requirement in the quality management approach, because independent quality assurance needs to be planned at the beginning of the project.

23. During stage 2, the 'recorded sample songs' will be delivered and made available to members of focus groups. Feedback from the focus groups will be used to improve the 'recorded album'. The production manager has asked the singer to assess the recordings of the sample songs. This has been planned as part of the quality management approach.

Why is this an appropriate action?

A The quality that the singer expects from the 'recorded sample songs' needs to be documented.

B The quality checking of the 'recorded sample songs' needs to be aligned with the incremental delivery approach.

C The acceptance criteria for the 'recorded sample songs' need to be prioritized by the singer.

D The acceptance criteria for the 'recorded album' could change as a result of recording the sample songs.

38. During stage 3, the 'artwork' has been completed. However, it does not fully meet the quality criteria requested by the singer and in the documented product description. The cost of corrective action will be £500 and will delay the project by a week. The team manager has discussed this issue with the graphic designer and the singer. It has been agreed that the 'artwork' is good enough and will be used as it is.

    Is this an appropriate approach to controlling change, and why?

    A Yes, because the 'artwork' is of acceptable quality and project delay will be avoided.

    B Yes, because the singer has agreed the revisions to his original quality criteria.

    C No, because the project board must agree any change to the quality criteria.

    D No, because corporate, programme management or the customer must approve an off-specification.

Progress

Here are three statements relating to the music album project.

In which management product (A–E) should this information be recorded?

Choose only one product for each statement. Each product can be used once, more than once, or not at all.

39. When producing the 'artwork', the graphic designer needs to inform the singer which images have been selected.

40. An incident at the recording studio caused a delay in recording the songs. However, this will be completed within time tolerance.

41. There were problems with the power supply at the recording studio throughout stage 2. It is recommended that the studio use an alternative power supply for future projects.

    A Work package.

    B Checkpoint report.

    C Highlight report.

    D End stage report.

    E Exception report.

42. In stage 2, the music lawyer is a team manager working on the draft contract for the singer. He usually sends an email to the project manager every two days summarizing the status of the work. No major progress is expected over the next week, so the project manager amends the work package to receive reports over the phone.

    Is this appropriate, and why?

    A Yes, because a checkpoint report can be event-driven.
    B Yes, because a checkpoint report can be an oral report.
    C No, because the reporting format cannot be changed during delivery.
    D No, because only an exception report can be an oral report.

43. During the 'starting up a project' process, the project manager was told that the production assistant will not be available for the first stage. This issue needs to be managed formally.

    Which management product should be used to record this issue, and why?

    A Daily log, because it should be used to formally manage issues throughout the project lifecycle.
    B Daily log, because the issue register is not created during the 'starting up a project' process.
    C Issue register, because it should be used to formally manage issues throughout the project lifecycle.
    D Issue register, because it should be used by the project manager to monitor issues on a regular basis.

PRINCE2 processes

Starting up a project

Here are three actions carried out during the 'starting up a project' process.

Which role (A–F) should carry them out?

Choose only one role for each action. Each role can be used once, more than once, or not at all.

44. Decide whether the production manager can take on the role of project manager, given the estimated time and effort involved.

45. Seek approval from corporate management that the investment of time and money in promoting the singer is justified.

46. Review the priority of the acceptance criteria for the 'album ready for launch'.
   - A Executive.
   - B Senior user.
   - C Senior supplier.
   - D Project manager.
   - E Project support.
   - F Project assurance.

47. The project manager is preparing the project brief. A previous project had an issue with a focus group member uploading sample songs to the internet without permission. The project manager has asked the record company's cyber security expert to draft a section for the project brief that identifies measures required to prevent this from happening again.

   Is this appropriate, and why?
   - A Yes, because the project brief should record any risks identified during the 'starting up a project' process.
   - B Yes, because potential security issues that apply to the project should be considered when developing the project brief.
   - C No, because it is sufficient to record the issue in the lessons log for the team manager of the focus groups to consider.
   - D No, because it is a serious issue that should be recorded in the issue register and managed formally.

Directing a project

Here are three actions that are carried out as part of the 'directing a project' process.

During which activity (A–E) should the action occur?

Choose only one activity for each action. Each activity can be used once, more than once, or not at all.

48. Approve the work completed to record the album and the forecast to complete the 'registered artwork' and 'launch event plan'.

49. Ensure that there will be sufficient reviews after the launch event to monitor that the album sales deliver the expected profit.

50. Approve the forecast that the expected album sales will exceed the production costs, which was refined when the project plan was created.

A Authorize initiation.

B Authorize the project.

C Authorize a stage or exception plan.

D Give ad hoc direction.

E Authorize project closure.

51. The project is approaching the end of stage 2. The project manager may need to consult the senior user and executive about planning the production of the 'artwork', and the 'recorded album'. As a result, the project manager has checked their availability for the following week.

    Is this appropriate as part of the 'give ad hoc direction' activity, and why?

    A Yes, because the project board should provide advice to the project manager when preparing exception reports.

    B Yes, because the need for the project board to provide informal advice to the project manager increases at the end of a stage.

    C No, because highlight reports should keep the project board informed without the need for other communications.

    D No, because applying the 'manage by exception' principle should allow for the efficient use of senior managers' time.

Initiating a project

Here are three actions that take place during the 'initiating a project' process.

Which theme (A–F) is being applied?

Choose only one theme for each action. Each theme can be used once, more than once, or not at all.

52. The project manager transfers the following statement: 'A similar singer may be working on another album, to be released at the same time' from the daily log.

53. The project manager documents the statement: 'Funding was secured from a youth development fund, which must be used to produce the initial sample recordings.'

54. The singer's agent checks the project initiation documentation to ensure that the singer's needs will be met.

    A Business case.

    B Organization.

    C Risk.

D Progress.

E Plans.

F Quality.

55. The project manager has recommended that a highlight report should be submitted every four weeks. However, as the project manager only joined the company recently, the executive wants to receive a highlight report every week while the sample songs are being recorded. As a result, the project manager has recorded this requirement in the controls section of the project initiation documentation.

Is this appropriate, and why?

A Yes, because the project board uses highlight reports to monitor progress during management stages.

B Yes, because the reporting should be more frequent when a team is inexperienced, to build confidence.

C No, because the frequency of highlight reports should be set in each stage plan to allow a different level of monitoring.

D No, because the frequency of highlight reporting should be specified in the communication management approach.

Controlling a stage

Here are three actions that are carried out during the 'controlling a stage' process.

During which activity (A–F) should each action be carried out?

Choose only one activity for each action. Each activity can be used once, more than once, or not at all.

56. The project manager updates the product description for the album cover, following a concession granted by the project board.

57. The project manager asks for confirmation from project support that the quality checks of the draft contract have been carried out, as reported in the checkpoint report.

58. The project manager asks project support to confirm the status of the sample songs, prior to preparing the regular progress report.

A Authorize a work package.

B Review work package status.

C Review the management status.

D Report highlights.

E Escalate issues and risks.

F Take corrective action.

59. An external recording studio will be used to record the sample songs from the start of stage 2. Therefore, the record company's purchasing department needs to carry out the supplier selection process during the initiation stage. The project manager has recommended that the 'controlling a stage' process is used to control the work of the purchasing department.

Is this appropriate, and why?

A Yes, because work packages should be used to manage work during the initiation stage.

B Yes, because using a work package will help to ensure that the output is delivered on time.

C No, because the 'controlling a stage' process should be used for work within delivery stages.

D No, because the team manager for the sample songs production should select the recording studio.

Managing product delivery

60. What should the recording studio manager do as part of the 'accept a work package' activity for the 'recorded album'?

A Agree when the 'recorded album' needs to be completed.

B Report the amount spent when producing the 'recorded album'.

C Verify that the required sound quality checks have been completed.

D Report progress on acceptance of the work package using a checkpoint report.

61. The team manager for the 'signed contracts for delivery channels' is in the process of accepting the work package. The team manager is concerned that the list of quality reviewers included in the product description may not include anyone with the required specialist knowledge.

What should the team manager do first?

A Consult with project assurance.

B Raise a risk with the project manager.

C Request a resource from the senior supplier.

D Revise the product description.

62. The project is in stage 2. The 'recorded sample songs' have been produced and handed over to the team manager for the focus groups. On the day before the focus group meeting, the team manager discovered that the sound quality of one song was not of the required standard. The team manager spoke to the singer's agent, and the singer will attend the focus group meeting to perform the songs.

    Is this appropriate application of the 'managing product delivery' process, and why?

    A Yes, because this will 'exploit' the opportunity for the focus group to hear the singer perform the songs.

    B Yes, because the team manager is taking corrective action to resolve the issue of the poor-quality recordings.

    C No, because the team manager should ask the recording studio manager to take corrective action.

    D No, because an issue should be raised so that the project manager can decide on corrective action.

Managing a stage boundary

63. The project is approaching the end of stage 3 and the 'artwork' is taking longer to produce than expected. As a result, an exception report has been sent to the project board. The project board has decided to follow the recommendation of the project manager to increase the time tolerance for the stage.

    When should the 'managing a stage boundary' process be used next?

    A When preparing the stage 4 plan for approval by the project board.

    B When reporting that stage 3 is now progressing according to plan.

    C When re-planning stage 3 in response to the increased time tolerance.

    D When the performance of the whole music album project is reviewed.

64. This project is part of a larger programme. An exception plan has been produced during the final stage because there has been a delay in the registering of the 'artwork'. The stage will be delayed; however, the project will be completed within the time tolerance set.

    Which role, or combination of roles, should approve this exception plan?

    A Programme board.

    B Project board.

C Project manager with project assurance.

D Both project board and programme board.

65. Late in stage 3, the project manager has reported that the 'artwork' is going to take longer to produce than planned, and the stage is likely to exceed time tolerance. As a result, the project board has requested an exception plan and also wants to establish the status of the current stage.

What action should the project manager take, and why?

A Prepare an exception report, because it should show the status of the work package.

B Prepare an exception report, because it should describe the options for dealing with the deviation.

C Prepare an end stage report, because the project board have asked what is outstanding for stage 3.

D Prepare an end stage report, because the project is nearing the end of stage 3.

Closing a project

66. Which action should the project manager take during the 'prepare planned closure' activity?

A Summarize the final amount spent in producing the 'recorded album', for future reference.

B Check the 'album ready for launch' to confirm that it meets the record company's requirements.

C Report on the number of downloads for the sample songs and the predicted sales.

D Identify the marketing activities that still need to take place to support the launch.

67. Which action should the project manager take during the 'hand over products' activity?

A Update the project plan with the actual time taken to plan the launch event.

B Check whether the graphic designer can be released to work on another project.

C Summarize whether the 'album ready for launch' was delivered on time and to cost.

D Review the dates when sales of the new album will be measured.

Q	A	Syllabus ref	Rationale	Further comments from the chief examiner
11	F	2.1.1b	F. **Correct**. Project assurance should monitor project finance on behalf of corporate, programme management or the customer. Ref Tab. 6.1 A, B, C, D, E. Incorrect. Ref Tab. 6.1	
12	D	2.1.2	A. Incorrect. The customer's business case should include all costs. However, the graphic designer's business justification should not be part of the project's business case. Ref A.2.2, 6.3.3 B. Incorrect. The customer's business case should include the benefits to the customer, but the graphic designer's business justification should not be part of the project's business case. Ref A.2.2, 6.3.3 C. Incorrect. It is true that where the project is part of the programme, the programme will typically define both the approach to business case development and provide an outline business case for the project. However, this does not explain why the supplier should have a separate business case. Ref 6.3.4 D. **Correct**. The project's business case for a customer's project is separate from a supplier's business justification for bidding for, and working on that customer's project. The customer needs to ensure that their project is viable and risks are acceptable, bearing in mind the suppliers chosen. A supplier would have to ensure that they will benefit from the work they undertake on the project. Ref 6.3.3	

Table continues

Practitioner exam sample paper rationale *continued*

Q	A	Syllabus ref	Rationale	Further comments from the chief examiner
13	D	2.1.2	A. Incorrect. Even though the singer's agent has experience of the market and skills to forecast sales, it is the senior user who specifies the benefits for the project. Ref Tab. 6.1 B. Incorrect. Even though the singer's agent understands the size of the market, it is the senior user who specifies the benefits for the project. Ref Tab. 6.1 C. Incorrect. The project manager is responsible for the development of the business case, but the benefits are specified by the senior user. Ref Tab. 6.1, C.5 D. **Correct**. The singer's agent is an external supplier who cannot be responsible for the benefits in the record company's business case. The senior user is accountable for specifying the benefits. Ref Tab. 6.1, C.3	
14	D	2.2.1c	D. **Correct**. The Marketing Department will use the product by marketing the album. The marketing manager is the right person to undertake the user assurance role by assessing whether the album meets the user's needs. Ref C.7.1, 7.2.1.5 A, B, C, E, F. Incorrect. Ref 7.1, C.5, C.7.1, C.9.1	
15	B	2.2.1c	B. **Correct**. The production manager has experience of managing album projects and, of the options that are provided, would be most appropriate for this role. Ref C.5 A, C, D, E, F. Incorrect. Ref 7.1, C.5, C.7.1, C.9.1	
16	C	2.2.1c	C. **Correct**. Provision of administrative support is one responsibility of project support. Ref C.9.1 A, B, D, E, F. Incorrect. Ref 7.1, C.5, C.7.1, C.9.1	

Q	A	Syllabus ref	Rationale	Further comments from the chief examiner
17	C	2.2.2	A. Incorrect. The recording studio manager is responsible for the delivery of the recorded album. However, business assurance should be undertaken by someone from the customer organization, to avoid a conflict of interest. Ref 7.2.1.10 B. Incorrect. Although the recording studio manager has the required knowledge and experience, the business assurance role should be undertaken by someone from the customer organization. The recording studio manager is a supplier and therefore this would be a conflict of interest. Ref 7.2.1.10 C. **Correct**. There may be conflict between customer and supplier business justification. The business assurance role should be undertaken by someone from the customer organization as the recording studio manager is a supplier. Ref 7.2.1.10 D. Incorrect. Ideally, those with project assurance responsibilities should be able to carry out the role throughout the project, although it is possible for someone to provide project assurance during a specific stage. This is not the reason why it is not appropriate for the recording studio manager to undertake the role. Business assurance should be undertaken by someone from the customer organization to avoid a conflict of interest. Ref 7.2.1.10, C.7.2	

Table continues

Practitioner exam sample paper rationale *continued*

Q	A	Syllabus ref	Rationale	Further comments from the chief examiner
18	A	2.2.2	A. **Correct**. The project manager can always choose to be the team manager. In a commercial environment, the supplier's staff may fulfil a team manager role on the project – this is not mandatory and can introduce a conflict of interest. Ref 7.2.1.8, 7.3.4 B. Incorrect. It is important that the project manager has a good understanding of the supplier contractual obligations in a commercial environment. However, this does not explain why the project manager and team manager roles may be combined in the situation described. Ref. 7.3.4 C. Incorrect. The graphic design company is a third-party supplier and there could be a reporting line between the team manager and the senior supplier. This link would need to be understood in order to avoid conflicts of interest. However, appointing the team manager from the third-party supplier would introduce the conflict of interest, not avoid it. Ref 7.2.1.8 D. Incorrect. The project manager should plan roles during the 'starting up a project' process. However, this does not explain why the project manager and team manager roles may be combined in the situation described. Ref 7.2.1.8, 14.4.3	

Q	A	Syllabus ref	Rationale	Further comments from the chief examiner
55	B	3.3.2	A. Incorrect. The project board does use highlight reports to monitor and control management stages and project progress, however this is not the reason why it is appropriate to set the frequency of the reports to weekly in this case, and record this information in the project initiation documentation (PID). Ref A.20.2, 16.4.6, 12.2.2.4, 19.4.1 B. **Correct**. It is in the PID that the frequency of the highlight reports for the duration of the project would be stated, with an understanding that for each stage in the stage plan the frequency for highlight reports would be agreed. Each stage may need a different level of control and more or less frequent reports. As the confidence in the project manager and team increases in future stage plans the board may agree to less frequent highlight reports. The PID will be updated to show this. Ref A.20.2, 16.4.6, 12.2.2.4, 19.4.1 C. Incorrect. It is appropriate to record the frequency of highlight reporting in the PID. It is true that each stage may need a different level of control and more or less frequent reports, but if the frequency of reporting changes, this would be reflected in both the stage plan for that change and in an update to the PID. Ref A.20.2, 16.4.6, 12.2.2.4, 19.4.1 D. Incorrect. The action described is appropriate. Additionally, although it is true that the communication management approach states when formal communication activities are to be undertaken (for example, at the end of a management stage) including performance audits of the communication methods, this does not explain why the frequency of reporting may be varied to take into account the inexperience of team members. Ref A.5.2, 12.2.2.4	
56	F	3.4.1a	F. **Correct**. The product description will need to be updated to reflect the concession granted by the project board. This is a corrective action that has been decided on, e.g. to resolve an issue with the 'artwork'. Ref. 17.4.8 A, B, C, D, E. Incorrect. Ref 17.4.1–8	

Table continues

Practitioner exam sample paper rationale *continued*

Q	A	Syllabus ref	Rationale	Further comments from the chief examiner
57	B	3.4.1a	B. **Correct**. Reviewing whether quality checks have been carried out, in the quality register, is part of the 'review the work package status' activity. Ref 17.4.2 A, C, D, E, F. Incorrect. Ref 17.4.1–8	
58	D	3.4.1a	D. **Correct**. A product status account can be requested to check the status of the products before reporting on progress, as part of the 'report highlights' activity. Ref. 17.4.5 A, B, C, E, F. Incorrect. Ref 17.4.1–8	
59	B	3.4.2	A. Incorrect. Work packages may be used during the initiation stage, but do not need to be used. Ref 17.3 B. **Correct**. The 'controlling a stage' process is normally first used after the project board authorizes the project, but it may also be used during the initiation stage, if necessary. Ref 17.3 C. Incorrect. The 'controlling a stage' process should be used for work within delivery stages. However, this is not the reason why it is appropriate to use the 'controlling a stage' process in the initiation stage in this context. Ref 17.3 D. Incorrect. The purchasing department is selecting the recording studio in this scenario. Team managers should be selected according to their capability to manage the work on the product. The team manager will be selected once the recording studio is selected. This product is not the responsibility of the sample song production team manager. Ref 7.2.1.8	

Q	A	Syllabus ref	Rationale	Further comments from the chief examiner
60	A	3.5.1a	A. **Correct**. The fundamental principle is that before a work package is allocated to a team, there should be agreement between the project manager and the team manager as to what is to be delivered. Ref 18.4.1 B. Incorrect. As part of the 'execute a work package' activity, the team manager should review and report the status of the work package to the project manager. Ref 18.4.2 C. Incorrect. As part of the 'deliver a work package' activity, the team manager should review the approval records to verify that all the products to be delivered by the work package are approved. Ref 18.4.3 D. Incorrect. Checkpoint reports are used to report progress in the 'execute a work package' activity, not as part of the 'accept a work package' activity. Ref 18.4.1, 18.4.2	
61	A	3.5.1a	A. **Correct**. When accepting a work package, the team manager should review the work package and consult with project assurance as to whether any extra reviewers are required. Ref 18.4.1 B. Incorrect. When accepting a work package, the team manager should review the work package and consult with project assurance as to whether any extra reviewers are required. If the concern cannot be resolved it may then be appropriate to raise a risk. Ref 18.4.1 C. Incorrect. When accepting a work package, the team manager should review the work package and consult with project assurance as to whether any extra reviewers are required. If it is agreed that a specialist reviewer is required, it may then be appropriate to ask the senior supplier for the resource. Ref 18.4.1 D. Incorrect. When accepting a work package, the team manager should review the work package and consult with project assurance as to whether any extra reviewers are required before any corrective action is taken. Ref 18.4.1	

Table continues

Practitioner exam sample paper rationale *continued*

Q	A	Syllabus ref	Rationale	Further comments from the chief examiner
62	D	3.5.2	A. Incorrect. The team manager can only proceed with the work package, or take corrective action, while the work package is forecast to be complete within the tolerances set by the project manager. Performing the songs live is outside the scope of the work package, so must be raised with the project manager to decide on corrective action. Deciding to 'exploit' the opportunity is not a decision the team manager should take. Ref 18.4.2, Tab. 10.3 B. Incorrect. The team manager can only proceed with the work package or take corrective action while the work package is forecast to complete within the tolerances set by the project manager. Therefore, it is not appropriate that the team manager decides to take this corrective action. Ref 18.4.2 C. Incorrect. The team manager can only proceed with the work package or take corrective action while the work package is forecast to complete within the tolerances set by the project manager. The recordings are off-specification and should be reported to the project manager via the issue process. Ref 18.4.2 D. **Correct**. The team manager can only proceed with the work package, or take corrective action, while the work package is forecast to be complete within the tolerances set by the project manager. Performing the songs live is outside the scope of the work package. Team managers must raise issues with the project manager before a decision is made to take corrective action. Ref 18.4.2	

Q	A	Syllabus ref	Rationale	Further comments from the chief examiner
63	A	3.6.1a	A. **Correct**. As the tolerance has been increased for the current stage, the next action to take would be corrective action. Therefore, the next use of the 'managing a stage boundary' process will be when planning the next stage. Ref 17.4.8, 19.4.1 B. Incorrect. As the tolerance has been increased for the current stage, the next action to take would be corrective action. Therefore, the next use of the 'managing a stage boundary' process will be when planning the next stage. Ref 17.4.8, 19.4.1 C. Incorrect. As part of the 'give ad hoc direction' activity, the project board can increase the tolerances that are forecast to be breached within their delegated limits of authority without the need for an exception plan. Therefore, the next use of the 'managing a stage boundary' process will be when planning the next stage. Ref 15.4.4, 19.4.1 D. Incorrect. Reviewing the performance of the whole project is done as part of the 'closing a project' process, not the 'managing a stage boundary' process. Ref 20.4.4	
64	B	3.6.1b	B. **Correct**. Exception plans must be produced to show the actions required to recover from or avoid a deviation from agreed tolerances in the project plan or a stage plan. If a stage plan is being replaced, this needs the approval of the project board. The exception plan has been produced for the final stage, so it must be submitted to the project board. The stage-level exception does not threaten project tolerance, so does not need to be referred to the programme level. Ref 9.2.1.3, Tab. 19.5 A, C, D – Incorrect. Ref 9.2.1.3, Tab. 19.5	

Table continues

Practitioner exam sample paper rationale *continued*

Q	A	Syllabus ref	Rationale	Further comments from the chief examiner
65	C	3.6.2	A. Incorrect. An exception report has already been produced. It is a checkpoint report that shows the status of work packages, not an exception report. The checkpoint report is produced by the team manager for the project manager during the 'managing product delivery' process. The project manager does not produce checkpoint reports. Ref Tab. 18.2, A.4.2, 19.4.4 B. Incorrect. An exception report has already been produced. The project board has requested an end stage report. Ref 19.4.4 C. **Correct**. If requested by the project board, an end stage report should be produced in response to the exception report and to accompany the exception plan. The end stage report will include the activities carried out to date. Ref 19.4.4 D. Incorrect. Although it is late in stage 3, an exception plan has been requested, along with an end stage report, because an exception has occurred, not because the project is approaching the end of stage 3. Ref 19.4.4	
66	B	3.7.1a	A. Incorrect. As part of the 'evaluate the project' activity, the project manager works with the project management team to summarize how the project has performed. Ref 20.4.4 B. **Correct**. As part of the 'prepare planned closure' activity, the project manager confirms that the project has delivered what is defined in the project product description and that the acceptance criteria have been met. Ref 20.4.1 C. Incorrect. As part of the 'evaluate the project' activity, the project manager completes an assessment of the project's results against the expected benefits in the business case within the end project report. Ref 20.4.4 D. Incorrect. As part of the 'hand over products' activity, the project manager prepares follow-on action recommendations to include any incomplete work, issues and risks. Ref 20.4.3	

Q	A	Syllabus ref	Rationale	Further comments from the chief examiner
67	D	3.7.1a	A. Incorrect. As part of the 'prepare planned closure' activity, the project plan is updated with actuals from the final management stage. Ref 20.4.1 B. Incorrect. As part of the 'prepare planned closure' activity, approval is requested to give notice to corporate, programme management or the customer that resources can be (or are about to be) released. Ref 20.4.1 C. Incorrect. As part of the 'prepare planned closure' activity, it is confirmed that the project has delivered what is defined in the project product description, and that the acceptance criteria have been met. Ref 20.4.1 D. **Correct**. As part of the 'hand over products' activity, the benefits management approach is checked to ensure that it includes post-project activities to confirm the benefits that cannot be measured until after the project's products have been in operational use for some time. Ref 20.4.3	
68	C	3.7.2	A. Incorrect. There are no lessons to be learned from the context given, so the information is not relevant when updating a lessons report or the end project report. Ref A.8.1, A.15.1 B. Incorrect. The follow-on action recommendations cover the project's products and include any uncompleted work, issues and risks. There are no follow-on actions identified in the context given. Ref 20.4.1, 20.4.3 C. **Correct**. Project support creates the product status account to check that the products, in this case the 'launch event plan', have been approved by the authority identified in the product description. Ref 20.4.1 D. Incorrect. Project support creates the product status account to check that the products, in this case the 'launch event plan', have been approved by the authority identified in the product description. Project support is not responsible for the support of products, so have no support to transfer. Ref 20.4.1, 20.4.3	Here you need to understand from the preamble that a product has been approved. This information has not led to any lessons; therefore A is incorrect. There are no outstanding issues, therefore there are no follow-on action recommendations which means that B is incorrect. D is also incorrect as project support does not transfer responsibility for the launch event plan. It is the project manager who obtains the acceptance record, not project support. Therefore, C is correct, as the product status account reports on the status of the products and is created by project support during the 'prepare premature closure' activity.

4

Maintaining your professional status

4 Maintaining your professional status

If you passed your PRINCE2 practitioner exam prior to the 2017 edition of the PRINCE2 manual, you will have to sit a full 2.5-hour PRINCE2 2017 practitioner exam.

If you are taking the exam in a language into which the 2017 edition has not yet been translated, you may be able to take a re-registration exam. This exam is an objective test exam with the following format:

- Three questions: 10 items per question, each worth 1 mark
- 17 or more marks required to pass (out of 30 available): 57%
- One hour's (60 minutes) duration, no additional reading time
- Open-book exam: only the official printed PRINCE2 manual is allowed.

Note that the guidance in this publication does not apply to this exam.

If you took the 2017 version of the PRINCE2 practitioner exam, you have two choices in order to maintain your professional status:

- Become a PRINCE2 member and maintain/log continuous professional development (CPD) points. See the AXELOS website for more information.
- Re-sit the full 2.5-hour practitioner exam within 3–5 years.

Figure 4.1 shows the various ways in which you can maintain your professional status.

To continue your PRINCE2 journey and connect with and join conversations with project management professionals, visit: https://www.axelos.com/community

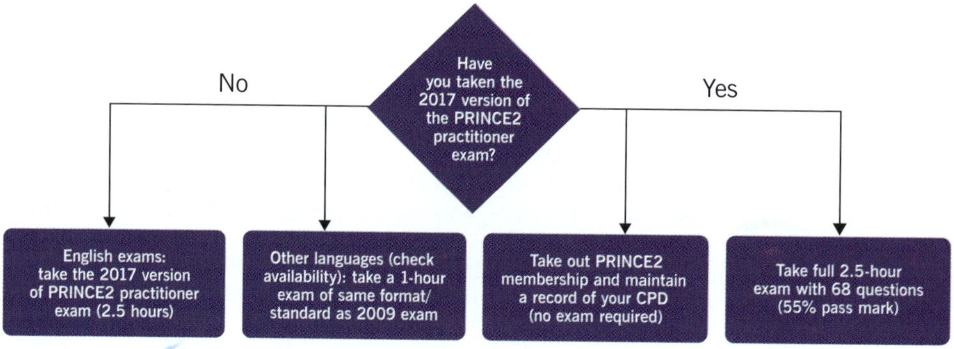

Figure 4.1 Maintaining your professional status

A

Instructions for taking the online foundation exam

Appendix A: Instructions for taking the online foundation exam

1. Purchase your exam from your chosen provider.
2. Create an account with PeopleCert.
3. Register for your exam using the voucher code supplied by your accredited organization.
4. Choose an exam date and time and book your exam.
5. You will receive a confirmation email to confirm your exam booking. You will receive a reminder email the day before your exam.
6. On the day of your exam, up to one hour before the exam start time, log on to your PeopleCert account. It will show that your exam is waiting for you. You will need to install or run Exam Shield. Once this is done, run a systems check using Exam Shield. This will require you to have your speaker/microphone and webcam switched on to test both audio and video. Display screen resolution will need to be set to 100% or 125%. Your internet connectivity will need to be good. It is recommended that you use a personal device rather than one that is connected via a company VPN.
7. Up to 10 minutes before the exam start time, close all other applications and you can start the exam registration process by clicking the 'Start' button. Note this does not start the exam, simply the exam administration.
8. First, you will be required to accept a non-disclosure agreement.
9. You will then be presented with exam instructions. Make sure you read these carefully.
10. If required, you can review the exam tutorial which will show you how to navigate through the exam.
11. You will then be presented with the exam rules which you will need to 'tick' to confirm you have understood them all.
12. You will be required to upload a copy of your photo ID. You can do this by uploading a saved file or using your webcam to take a photo.

13. A details verification screen will now appear, but you will not be able to proceed until the exam proctor joins you by chat and audio.
14. The exam proctor will ask you to use your webcam to show them the room and that you have put your mobile phone out of your reach, but on silent.
15. Once the exam proctor is satisfied, you will be able to confirm that your details are correct by clicking the 'Next' button on the details verification screen.
16. You can minimize the chat window by clicking on the red arrow on the left-hand side of the window. You can open it again at any time if you need assistance from the exam proctor.
17. If you are ready, click the 'Start Exam' button. The timer will now start to count down and the first question will be displayed.
18. Please note that:
    - Questions turn orange when you have selected an answer.
    - You can flag a question to review it later by clicking on the flag button on the far left-hand side of the screen. You can do this either after you have selected an answer or without selecting an answer. It is strongly recommended that you always select an answer for a question even if you change the answer when you review it.
    - If you do not select an answer for a question but move to the next question, the question will not turn orange.
    - The previous/next buttons are at the top of the screen on the right-hand side.
    - The End Exam button is at the bottom right of the screen. If you click on this by accident it will ask whether you are sure you want to end the exam. If you wish to continue, you should select 'no'.
    - At the top left-hand side of the screen it will tell you how many questions you have answered out of 60. The count-down timer is at the top right of the screen.
    - You can go back to the previous question at any time using the 'Previous' button.
    - You can review any question at any time, simply by clicking on the question number in the left-hand margin.
    - You can 'unflag' a question which you have reviewed by clicking on the black flag.
19. Once you have selected an answer for every question – the question should have turned orange – review any flagged questions to make sure you are happy with your original answer. Make any changes required, but beware of changing your answer without a good reason!

20. If you are ready to end your exam, click the end 'End Exam' button. You will be asked to confirm that you want to end the exam. Click 'OK'.
21. You will be taken to a short survey about the exam process. Once you have completed the survey you will then be given your exam result after you click on 'Submit and show my results'.
22. You will be shown your overall score and the breakdown of your score by syllabus area.
23. You should uninstall Exam Shield after completing your exam.
24. Your official results will be emailed to you and your certificate will be available on your PeopleCert account within two working days.

Please note that some of these steps, such as installing Exam Shield, may have already been completed by your accredited organization if you are using a device supplied by them. In addition, the classroom-based invigilator will take the role of the exam proctor.

Figure A.1 provides a screenshot of the layout you can expect to see when taking your online exam.

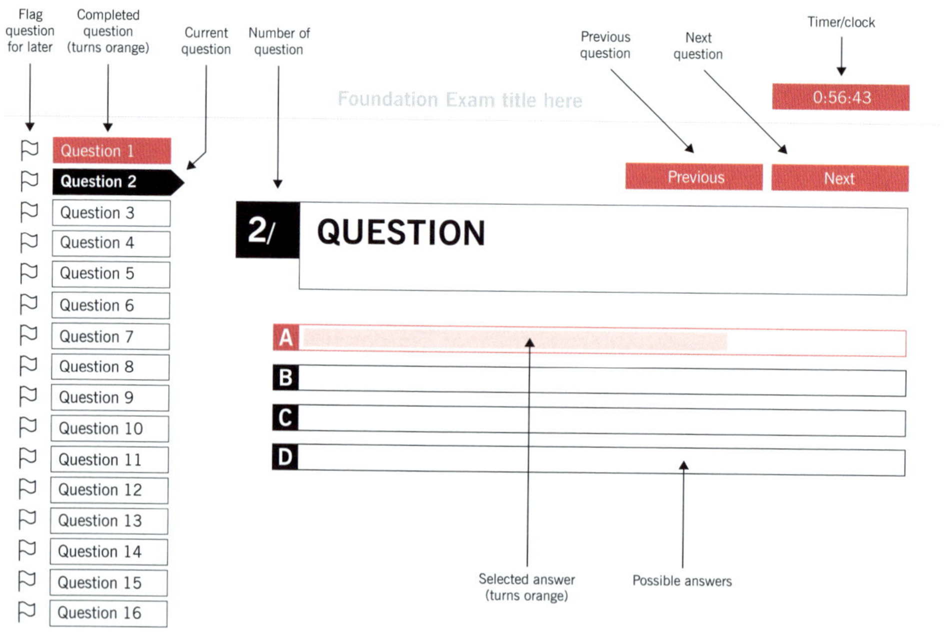

Figure A.1 Screen layout for the online foundation exam

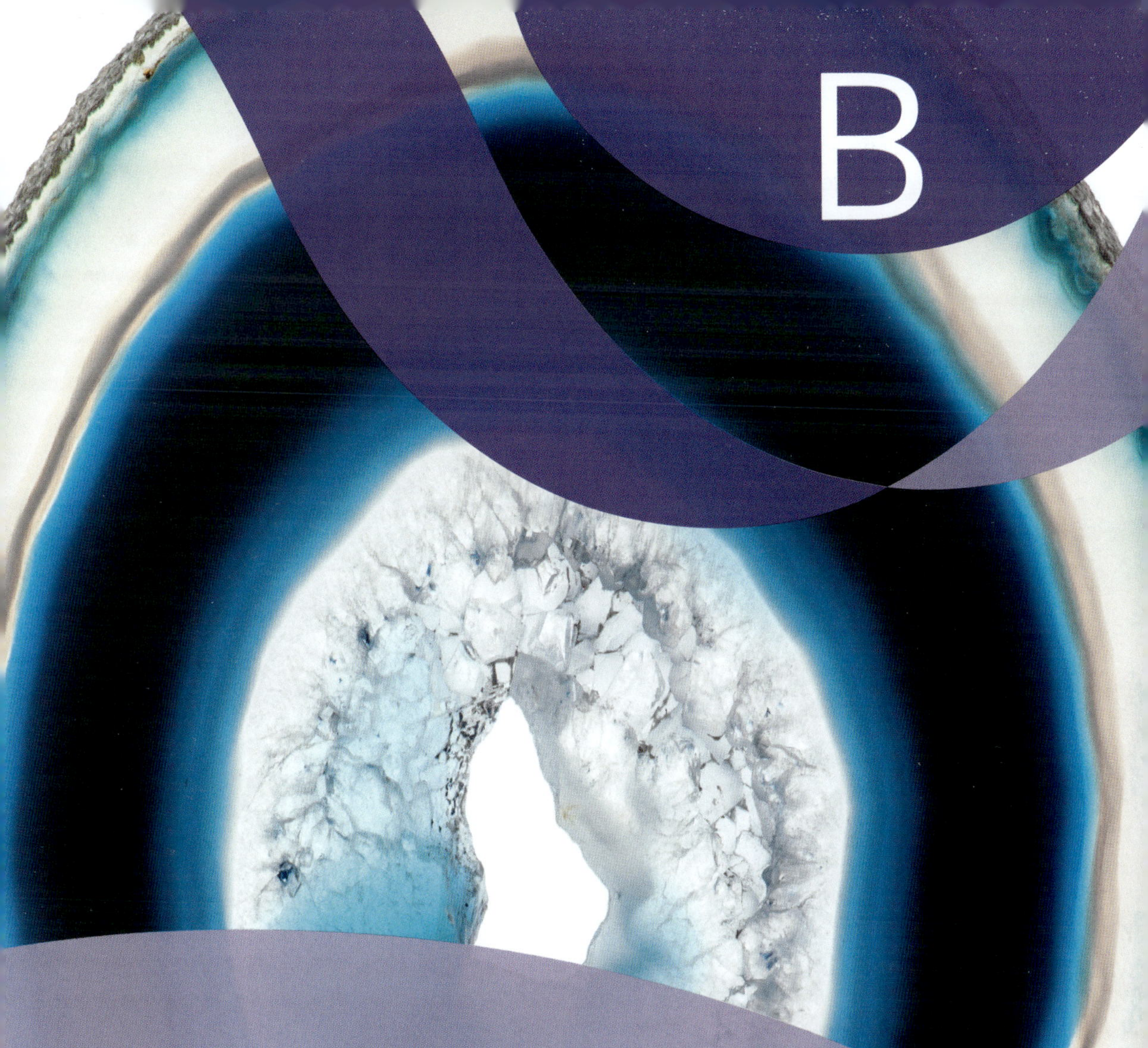

B

Instructions for taking the online practitioner exam

Appendix B: Instructions for taking the online practitioner exam

1. Purchase your exam from your chosen provider.
2. Create an account with PeopleCert, or log in to your account if you already have one from when you took your foundation exam.
3. Register for your exam using the voucher code supplied by your accredited organization.
4. Upload any prerequisites (foundation certificate) if not already shown on your PeopleCert profile page.
5. Choose an exam date and time and book your exam.
6. You will receive a confirmation email to confirm your exam booking and a reminder email the day before your exam.
7. On the day of your exam, up to one hour before the exam start time, log on to your PeopleCert account. It will show that your exam is waiting for you. You will need to install or run Exam Shield. Once this is done, run a systems check using Exam Shield. This will require you to have your speaker/microphone and webcam switched on to test both audio and video. Display screen resolution will need to be set to 100% or 125%. Your internet connectivity will need to be good. It is recommended that you use a personal device rather than one that is connected via a company VPN.
8. Up to 10 minutes before the exam start time, close all other applications and you can start the exam registration process by clicking on the 'Start' button. Note this does not start the exam, simply the exam administration.
9. First, you will be required to accept a non-disclosure agreement.
10. You will then be presented with exam instructions. Make sure you read these carefully.
11. If required, you can review the exam tutorial which will show you how to navigate through the exam.

12. You will then be presented with the exam rules which you will need to 'tick' to confirm you have understood them all.
13. You will be required to upload a copy of your photo ID. You can do this by uploading a saved file or using your webcam to take a photo.
14. A details verification screen will now appear, but you will not be able to proceed until the exam proctor joins you by chat and audio.
15. The exam proctor will ask you to use your webcam to show them the room and that you have put your mobile phone out of your reach, but on silent.
16. Once the exam proctor is satisfied, you will be able to confirm that your details are correct by clicking the 'Next' button on the details verification screen.
17. You can minimize the chat window by clicking on the red arrow on the left-hand side of the window. You can open it again at any time if you need assistance from the exam proctor.
18. If you are ready, click the 'Start Exam' button. The timer will now start to count down and the first question will be displayed.
19. Please note that:
    - You should read the scenario and additional information by clicking on the button at the top right of the screen. This will open in a separate window and you can select whether to open the scenario or the additional information. Click on the 'Close' button and you will now be able to maximize the scenario or additional information below each question.
    - Questions turn orange when you have selected an answer.
    - You can flag a question to review it later by clicking on the flag button on the far left-hand side of the screen. You can do this either after you have selected an answer or without selecting an answer. It is strongly recommended that you always select an answer for a question even if you change the answer when you review it.
    - If you do not select an answer for a question but move to the next question, the question will not turn orange.
    - The previous/next buttons are at the top of the screen on the right-hand side.
    - The End Exam button is at the bottom right of the screen. If you click on this by accident it will ask you whether you are sure you want to end the exam. If you wish to continue, you should select 'no'.

- At the top left-hand side of the screen it will tell you how many questions you have answered out of 46. The count-down timer is at the top right of the screen. Note that it shows the total number of questions to be answered as 46 rather than 68 as the matching questions are shown as one question, although they are marked as three separate sub-questions.
- You can go back to the previous question at any time using the 'Previous' button.
- You can review any question at any time, simply by clicking on the question number in the left-hand margin.
- You can 'unflag' a question which you have reviewed by clicking on the black flag.

20. The syllabus area being examined is shown above the FIRST question within that syllabus area and not repeated above each question. You should therefore note every time the syllabus area changes.
21. For questions in the matching format, you will need to drag the options from the right-hand side of the screen on to the question on the left-hand side of the screen. Note that you can change your mind by dragging an alternative answer on to the question.
22. Once you have selected an answer for every question – the question should have turned orange – review any flagged questions to make sure you are happy with your original answer. Make any changes required, but beware of changing your answer without a good reason!
23. If you are ready to end your exam, click the end 'End Exam' button. You will be asked to confirm that you want to end the exam. Click 'OK'.
24. You will be taken to a short survey about the exam process. Once you have completed the survey you will then be given your exam result after you click on 'Submit and show my results'.
25. You will be shown your overall score and the breakdown of your score by syllabus area.
26. You should uninstall Exam Shield after completing your exam.
27. Your official results will be emailed to you and your certificate will be available on your PeopleCert account within two working days.

Figure B.1 provides a screenshot of the layout you can expect to see when answering a standard multiple choice question in your online exam, while Figure B.2 shows the layout for a matching question. Please note that some of these steps, such as installing Exam Shield, may have already been completed by your accredited organization if you are using a device supplied by them. In addition, the classroom-based invigilator will take the role of the exam proctor.

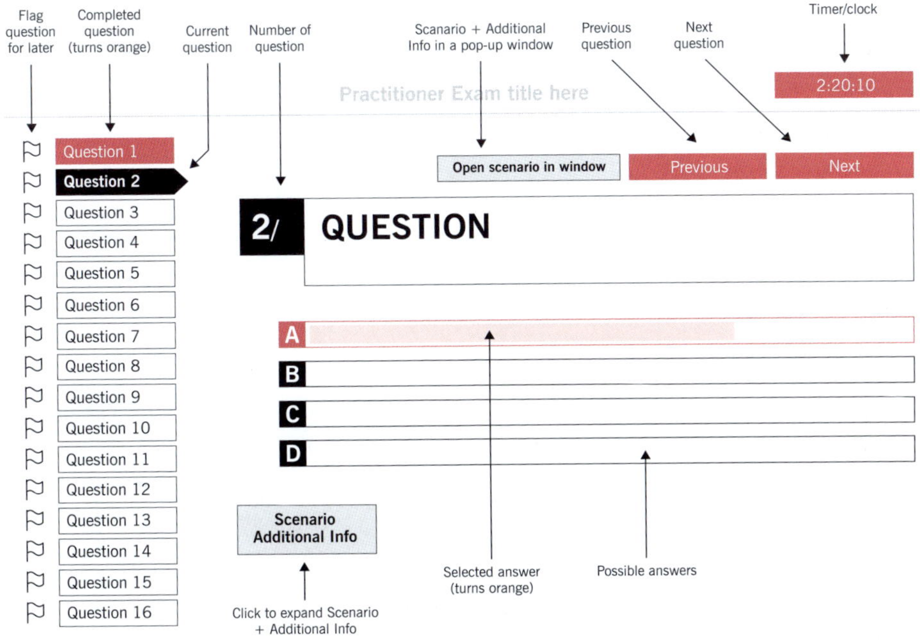

Figure B.1 Screen layout for the online practitioner exam (standard multiple choice question)

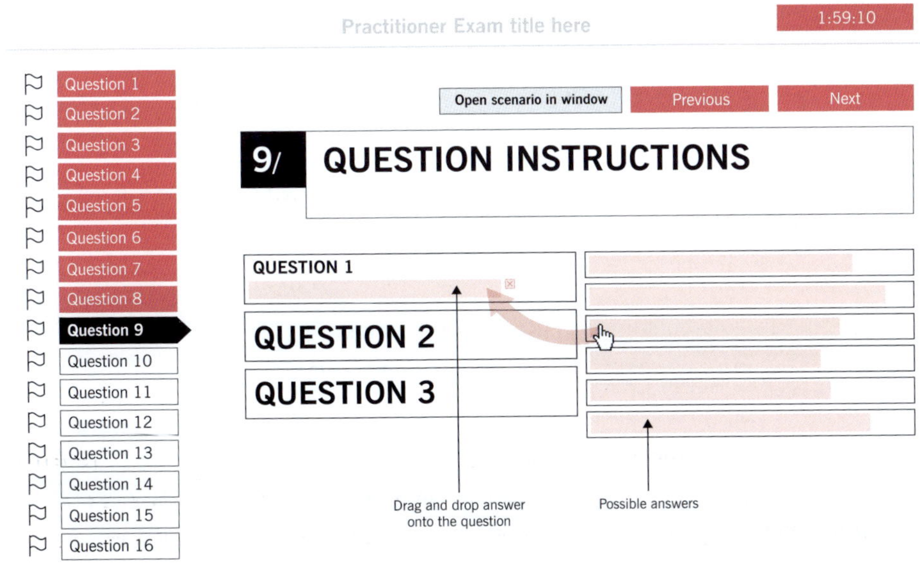

Figure B.2 Screen layout for the online practitioner exam (matching question)